しとどがふ従に形の影

IN

THE

SHADOW

OF

TRINITY

しとどがふ従に形の影

IN
THE
SHADOW
OF
TRINITY

AN AMERICAN AIRMAN
IN OCCUPIED JAPAN

Robert V. Vaughn

Sunflower University Press®

1531 Yuma (Box 1009), Manhattan, Kansas 66502-4228 USA

Cover photo, Fujiyama, by Fritz Henle, 1936.
Used with permission.

ISBN 0-89745-140-6

Edited by Sonie Liebler
Layout by Lori L. Daniel

*This small work is
humbly dedicated to
My adopted Japanese Father*

The Honorable Kunetoshi Tsugumo

Contents

Preface   ix

Foreword   xv

Acknowledgment   xvii

Chapter 1   Youth — Before Military Service   1

Chapter 2   World War II — Military Training   3
Induction — Ft. Hayes, Ohio — Coastal Artillery,
Anti-Aircraft Basic Training — Army Air Corps
Cadet Basic Training — College Training Detach-
ment — Classification — Pre-Flight Training —
Primary Flight Training — Basic Flight Training —
Advanced Flight Training — Graduation - Pilot —
B-24 Transition Training — Crew and Theater
Assignments — Departure from the United States

Chapter 3   Foreign Service — Prior to Peace   27
Embarkation — Philippine Islands — Ie Shima —
Air Attacks — Bombing Missions — Atomic
Bomb — Paper Bombs — Surrender — Air Cargo
Transport

Chapter 4   Japan — Occupation Service   59
Occupation Duty — Yokota — C-46 Curtiss Com-
mando — Flight to Biak, New Guinea — Russian
Threat — Tachikawa

Chapter 5   **Japan — Occupation Discoveries**   76
             Discovering Japan — Transportation and Distance
             — The Role of Tea in Japan — Fujiyama — My
             First Japanese Discoveries - Fussa and Ome —
             Tokyo — Mitaka — Tachikawa — Religion —
             Hachioji — Hanno — Hino — Other Matters —
             Parting Shot

Chapter 6   **Japan — The House of Tsugumo**   117
             Papa Kunetoshi Tsugumo — Background — Initial
             Encounter — Music — Musical Drama — Movies
             — Artwork — Fishing — History — Other Events
             — Personal Notes — In Retrospect

Chapter 7   **Return to the United States**   160
             The Voyage Home — Ft. Sheridan, Illinois —
             Terminal Leave

Epilogue   166
             Flying and Aircraft — The Japanese People — Atomic and
             Nuclear Bombs

Select Bibliography   169

Publications by Robert V. Vaughn   172

Index   174

Preface

Kage no katachi ni shitagoga gotoshi

As the shadow follows the substance.

Midzukami
*A Collection of Japanese
Proverbs and Sayings*

The meaning of the title, *In the Shadow of Trinity,* may be obvious to some, and not so obvious to others. It was selected because my entire life and military career (albeit very short) was affected by greater developments than the "mere" fighting of a war, not to mention my infinitesimal part in that "great war." Those greater developments involved the production of the atomic bomb. The first atomic bomb, the Fat Man, was detonated on 16 July 1945 at its test site named "Trinity" in New Mexico.

I was, at that time, all of 20 years of age and was stationed at Hamilton Field in California, awaiting air transportation to the Asiatic/Pacific war zone. We departed from Hamilton Field the next day, 17 July 1945, and we did not even really know that we were in the shadow of Trinity.

The quotation from Midzukami might better be translated as, "The shadow is inseparable from the light" — the symbolic connection to the atomic bomb may not be so obvious. In my case, the quotation might also have been restated as, "The shadow that follows the overwhelming light of the feeling of Ohn." That feeling of "Ohn" is the inner response an individual has for another individual or group of individuals because of some mental, spiritual, familial, or material debt. I had such a feeling for Kunetoshi Tsugumo and his family, who gave me such a marvelous short life in Japan with them.

I collected and retained many photographs, negatives, and other items from

World War II, in anticipation of publishing this volume. It was from this material that I began writing. Part of my narrative is based upon recollection, of course, but also upon three primary sources: correspondence written to my parents, a diary concerning Stateside service, and a monograph which I published in 1969, *An American Airman's Experiences in Post-War Japan (1945-1946)*. This monograph was written in 1946 and 1947 and reflected the view and "expertise" of a high school graduate of 22 and 23 years, prior to entering Ohio State University, instead of that of the 45-year-old man who published it for the first time in 1969. Contrast that with the fact that this present volume is written and compiled by a 66-year-old man.

In November 1945, Miss Thrall, the librarian of the Dorcas Carey Public Library, suggested to my mother that she wanted to publish the correspondence I had sent home. I was a prolific letter writer. During my foreign service, I know that I wrote at least 39 letters to my mother and my father alone from 16 July 1944 through 14 July 1945, because they saved that number. There were many other letters which I wrote to other members of the family, to former teachers and friends. I suggested, however, that it might be better to edit these, for they included much that was very personal, and which would not necessarily be of interest to others.

As a youth, I had spent countless hours in the library, and my idol, Miss Thrall, guided me through some great hours there, opening up new worlds. Perhaps now I am fulfilling her wish.

The final impetus for writing this account came during visits to my home by Fritz Henle, the noted international photographer (for *Life, Fortune, The New York Times, Harper's Bazaar*, and others). It was during the post-Hurricane Hugo time in 1989-1990, when my phone was operative while most other communication was not, that Mr. Henle visited me to use my line. Mr. Henle, I learned, had published an excellent photographic treatise in 1937 on prewar Japan, *Das Ist Japan*, published by Heering-Verlag. There was even one photograph in that volume, "The Toho Theatre," for which I had a corresponding photograph taken after the war. Upon discussing my experiences in Japan with Mr. Henle, I asked him for an opinion on whether my old negatives and prints were in a condition from which prints could be made. Although the negatives had been carefully preserved in protective envelopes away from light, heat, and moisture as far as possible, storage for the past 25 years on the Caribbean island of St. Croix is not the most ideal environment for photographic materials.

At first, Mr. Henle was somewhat skeptical, but ultimately assisted me by forwarding them to one of his professional photographic services to make contact prints as a test. The director of that service, Mr. Jeff Rowe, almost miraculously reproduced them, and subsequently made most of the prints which are being used in this publication.

Recently, while discussing this proposed project with a friend, she asked why I would want to do it — a very telling question. In essence, I replied that the studies relating to World War II generally have not been the eyewitness account of an 18- to 22-year-old participant. In addition, I said I also wanted to do it for reasons of vanity. And there were others. The first one became evident around 1971 when a friend, Carol Smith (of Estate Carleton in Frederiksted, St. Croix), who had spent some time in Japan after the war, asked to read my monograph. Her response after reading it was enlightening: "I found it most interesting, although the editor in me itched to correct misspellings." She concluded: "I'd like to see you expand the monograph if you can find time. It could be a book that fills in gaps." So, perhaps, I am fulfilling her wish also. Another reason surfaced when I gave a lecture to seventh and eighth graders at Good Hope School, perhaps in 1975 or 1976. I was told by a 13- or 14-year-old student, "Well, I hope you are proud of yourself for bombing innocent women and children." That was disturbing and was one of the primary reasons to write this memoir.

Some military terms are vague in my mind and are used as I remember them, not necessarily as they were and/or are, and certainly not as some of them have developed to date. There may be some confusion with the terms "U.S. Army Air Corps," "U.S. Army Air Forces," and "U.S. Air Force." In general, I have used the first term in relation to Aviation Cadet training; the second term more or less in relation to the post-Cadet period; and the last one the present period.

The spelling of Japanese words was a problem. My usage is sometimes the phonetic, which I devised while in Japan, with no Japanese-English, English-Japanese dictionaries available nor sources which delineated phonetic spellings for Japanese words. Spellings differed in my own diary, my correspondence, and in my monograph. In addition, I have found different spellings in sources, atlases, etc., which were available to me. Rather than attempt to uniformly change all names, generally I have elected to retain my usage at the time. That in itself should be of interest to linguists. In 1945 I had no knowledge about the International Phonetic Alphabet. Therefore, I have elected to overlook any spelling variations.

I have taken primarily a retrospective photojournalistic approach. As such, images from negatives which are 50 years old or older have been resurrected and are being used to channel my review. Negatives had to be made of some of the original images in order to prepare them for publication. The failings of making prints from 50-year-old negatives and especially from yellowed prints (taken by an inexperienced person, with a very inexpensive fixed-lens camera, with film of doubtful vintage at time of exposure, and development of doubtful nature), left much to be desired. However, the story, in this author's view, is important enough that the quality of the photographs should not determine its suitability for publication. It is to record history, rather than to display photographic competence and quality, that this memoir is published.

The paucity of photos of B-24 Liberator Bombers will become noticeable. This has resulted, not by design. One reason was that I had removed a number of photos of my crew and myself with B-24s from my photo album when making presentations to students relating to World War II, and some of them disappeared. I did not have any overall views of a B-24 Liberator, but through the courtesy of General Dynamics, I was able to obtain the copy included in Chapter 3. I also did not have any photos of the AT-10 twin-engine advanced trainer. Through the courtesy of Beech Aircraft I was able to obtain a copy of this handsome aircraft (Chapter 2). Photos of the BT-13 Vultee Valiant were also not in my collection, but again General Dynamics came to the rescue (Chapter 2).

Subsequently, other resources and photographs were discovered missing or were destroyed during and after Hurricane Hugo. More significant, however, is that photographing the B-24 in foreign arenas would have been desirable, but we were generally advised not to take photographs in the war zone.

There are no photos of some bases where I was stationed nor of some individual airplanes, nor of some crews with whom I flew, because either I did not have a camera or film at the time, or it was prohibited, or it was not convenient to do so.

My final reason is that there was a shortage of film (I suppose because the taking of photographs which might reveal any information to the enemy was not to be encouraged). That shortage made photography very precious. In addition, usually film could not be developed and would either have to be "smuggled" home for developing, or the "black market" would have to be used (sometimes through the base photographic section, reserved for official and reconnaissance photography). This resulted in film becoming "lost in the mail," damaged in the mail, or damaged in processing. I know of several rolls of film mailed home which never reached their destination, for I wrote to my family: "You will remember those rolls of film I sent home, well I only received two of the pictures. . . ."

No significant amount of extensive research has been expended in this work. Instead, the author's personal letters written to family members, diaries, correspondence received, and such have been utilized. Much of what is written is from this author's memory. As such, the resulting story is either from "the way it was," "the way I saw it," or "the way I wanted to see it." As a result, it is not necessarily an unbiased account.

Although I did not explain it to anyone before, and, in fact, I was not exactly positive of it myself, my desire to write this obviously was also because of the overwhelming feeling of Ohn, to include the relationship with my Japanese family. It is primarily for the purpose of filling in recorded history "gaps" and to fulfill obligations that I am finally publishing this — although vanity does have its place. Which reason has been the major factor, readers will have to decide.

Robert V. Vaughn, Ed.D.
Christiansted, St. Croix, V.I.

Foreword

The big passenger ship *Conte Verde* of the Lloyd Trestino line had carried me through the Suez Canal into the Indian Ocean. I was on my way to Japan, a fabulous multi-island nation, which I knew from the stories of my father and the art treasures he had brought home. He had been the Director of the Red Cross, stationed in Tokyo during the war with Russia in 1905. The Emperor, being appreciative of his services, granted him some fabulous gifts. I thought I was well prepared for my arrival, knowing much of the Islands from the beautiful photographs my father had taken.

In 1935 there was yet no air travel. On the beautiful *Conte Verde*, the trip would last four weeks. The long stops in Bombay and Colombo had broken the monotony which lay before us, with the next destination being Shanghai. Mountainous seas and powerful fierce winds seemed to prevent the proud liner from ever reaching the big Chinese metropolis. It was a typhoon which assaulted us without any advanced warning. Suddenly we found ourselves in its power — ready to destroy our ship and our lives. We had trusted its strong construction, its gracious lines, and its speed to cover the tremendous distance carrying us into a fabulous new world. For days our fate seemed sealed as we drifted almost helplessly, being tossed around in this violent storm. Nobody was to be seen but the brave men on the bridge and in the engine room. They fought a valiant battle and it was like a miracle, when the skies cleared again and we found ourselves in the safe harbor of Shanghai. Only a few days later we arrived on the battered ship in Yokohama.

On the horizon, faintly I could see a beautiful white peak. From my father's pictures, I realized this must be the sacred mountain, FUJIYAMA. From that moment on, I felt as if I were drawn by a magnet. I was compelled to get close to this beautiful white peak as soon as possible. After the turbulent days in the China Seas, this image seemed to me like nature's personification of peace and beauty and strength. I wandered by foot, and the closer I got, the more my fascination grew, compounded by the perfect image of the mountain. The people who lived in its shadow shared their devotion with me — the newcomer whose language they did not understand. But it was the common belief, our awe for the powerful vista of the mountain, which bound us together.

When I was honored to give some of my knowledge to my friend Bob Vaughn in creating his work and sharing his sensitive experiences, I realized that our human race with all its faults could not overcome the magic symbol of powerful beauty and everlasting peace — *Mount Fuji — Fujiyama*.

Fritz Henle
Written on Princess Hill
above Christiansted,
St. Croix
30 August 1990

Acknowledgment

Many persons have contributed to the potential for creating this volume. I must first acknowledge the important contributions of my Japanese family, the Tsugumo family, and especially Taro Kikutani. In addition, I gratefully acknowledge my mother, Ellen Haffey (Vaughn) Piska, who lovingly and carefully saved much of my correspondence.

Thanks should also go to Fritz Henle who encouraged me to prepare this memoir, in spite of the obvious poor quality of the photography, but who recognized its integrity, and who was the medium through which the old negatives and images were resurrected into reality. Thanks go, in addition, to Austin Prints for Publication, Austin, TX, for the careful attention and photographic technical expertise in transforming negatives and images into reality.

My own brother, Jim Vaughn, encouraged me to create this narrative, and he also assisted in editing it. In addition, I recognize that my brother, Joe Vaughn, was the photographer for one or two of the better photos. He, along with his wife, Mary, also assisted in the editing. Recognition is also extended to my sister, Margie Baron, my sister-in-law, Mary Lou Vaughn, and my brother Paul Vaughn, who were instrumental in retrieving and preserving copies of correspondence and photos which otherwise might have disappeared upon sale of the family farm and home in Carey, Ohio. The assistance of many others should also be acknowledged. I hope they will forgive me for not specifically including their names.

Vaughn family portrait (Robert Vaughn, back row, l.).

Chapter 1

Youth — Before Military Service

There is properly no history; only biography.

Ralph Waldo Emerson
Essays [First Series], 1841

I was born on a farm near Carey, Ohio, in November 1924 of Irish, Swiss, and apparently American Indian parentage. My father was born in Ohio, moved to Oklahoma as a young boy, and later moved back to Ohio. My mother was born in Nebraska and moved to Ohio upon her marriage to my father, whom she met while he was in military service in Kansas during World War I. There were five children in the family: James, Joseph, myself, Marjorie, and Paul (born about 13 years later). James was an engineer on a B-24 serving in Africa and Europe, and Joseph was a navigator on a B-17 serving in England.

I attended parochial elementary school and then, in 1938, attended public high school, taking a college preparatory course.

I recall vividly that I was a senior in high school and I was at a cinema in Findlay, Ohio, when news of Japan's attack upon Pearl Harbor greeted us. It was on Sunday afternoon, 7 December 1941. A classmate (Rex Houston, I believe) and I were confronted with this news as we emerged from the theater in the late afternoon (I do not recall the movie, for it was overshadowed by the news). That shock changed my attitude about World War II, and led to my eventual enlistment, induction, training, wartime experience, and postwar occupation of Japan. I was rather a pacifist in my early high school years and even when I was selected as a Junior Kiwanian in about 1940. In my speech to them I spoke against war and quoted the World War I anti-war poet Sigfried Sassoon's "The Aftermath."

Robert V. Vaughn, graduate of Carey High School, June 1942, in front of the family farmhouse near Carey, Ohio. (Photo by Ellen Vaughn with Kodak box camera.)

World War II stunned us all! Life and future planning changed. Here was a 17-year-old preparing to go to college with little incentive to pursue high school studies, much less college. I did, however, complete high school in 1942 with rather good grades and enrolled in Indiana Technical College in Radio/Electrical Engineering. The choice of a two-year college and this course of study were made as a result of personal interest and the fact of war and immediate demand for people with such training. Well, I might just as well have gone anywhere, and studied anything, for it was in 1942 that my actual military career started, on 11 December, almost on the first anniversary of Pearl Harbor.

Chapter 2

World War II — Military Training

Off We Go, into the Wild Blue Yonder . . .

Air Force Song

Induction

I was inducted into military service as a result of having signed up for the Army's Enlisted Reserve Corps (ERC), on 11 December 1942, about three weeks after having reached the "ripe old age" of 18. The ERC had obliquely promised that we would be able to complete college prior to being inducted. Shortly after enlisting, however, I heard rumors that we were all going to be inducted. It was then that I decided to take tests to enter the Army Air Corps Cadet program, because it would take precedence over the Regular Army. If I had to go into service, I would rather be in the Air Corps, and rather be an officer, and rather be a pilot!

In the Aviation Cadet physical exam, it was discovered that I was suffering from eye-strain from my studies and work. As a result, I went to an "eye doctor" who specialized in working with people who had eye strain. He used machines to exercise the eye muscles. It was hard work, but it was effective, and subsequently I passed all of the tests well beyond minimum requirements.

In my journey through the Army training in the United States, I was stationed in Ft. Hayes, Ohio (for assignment); Ft. Eustis, Virginia (Coastal Artillery basic training); Miami Beach, Florida (Air Corps basic training); Springfield College, Massachusetts (College Training Detachment); Nashville, Tennessee (Classification: Pilot, Navigator, or Bombardier, or —);

Private Vaughn with Andrews Sisters, 1943, Ft. Hayes, Ohio.

Maxwell Field, Alabama (Pre-Flight School); Darr Aero Tech, Albany, Georgia (Primary Flight Training in PT-13 Stearman by Boeing); Bush Field, Augusta, Georgia (Basic Flight Training in the BT-13 Vultee Valiant, or more popularly known as "Vultee Vibrator"); and Moody Field, Georgia (Advanced Flight Training in the AT-10, a trainer by Beech Aircraft). At the time I was in service, almost all pilot cadets went through eight phases: Basic Training, College Training Detachment (for those not having two years of college — a requirement to be an officer), Classification, Pre-Flight, Primary Flight Training, Basic Flight Training, Advanced Flight Training, and Transition.

Ft. Hayes, Ohio

My actual active service began at Ft. Hayes, Ohio. I recall vividly my mother taking me to the Big Four train station in Carey, Ohio, smilingly saying goodbye — albeit with uncontrollable tears in her eyes, and me with a lump in my throat. For several days while undergoing tests and "tailoring," we lived in our civilian clothes. One of the biggest problems we had was protecting the small cache of money we came with, for Uncle Sam gave no advances. There were incidents of people losing wallets while sleeping, while taking showers, etc. As result we slept warily with our wallets under our pillows. Think of it; where could you "hide" your money in a barracks room with 20 or 30 other persons, with no locks for footlockers, merely your luggage?

I was lucky. I don't remember how much money I came with, but it could not have been much more than $50, for I was a student up until induction, working two low-paying jobs (a bus-boy at Miller's Cafeteria primarily for meals, and a packer and elevator operator at Sears, Roebuck in Ft. Wayne, Indiana), while paying my own full tuition, room, and board.

During the time at Ft. Hayes, we learned that the Andrews Sisters (the hottest musical group in the U.S. at that time) were to visit the base. I lined up early — very early. During my youth, growing up on a farm near a small country town in Ohio, I had had very little opportunity to attend musical events with famous musicians, and I did not want to miss this opportunity. My greatest musical memory up until that time was having attended a concert featuring light operetta composer Sigmund Romberg while attending Indiana Technical College. My early arrival paid off, for I obtained a seat very close to the stage. I was in my glory. As a result of being in the right place at the right time, I had my picture taken by Army photographers with the three Andrew Sisters in one picture and in another with one of them (believe it or not, I can't remember which one) sitting on my lap — imagine!

Coastal Artillery, Anti-Aircraft Basic Training

Finally, on 17 April 1943, we were assigned to our branches of service at Ft. Hayes. To my consternation, I was not assigned to the Air Corps, even though I had documents advising that I was to be assigned to that branch. The documents were ignored by the military authorities. Instead, I was assigned to the Coastal Artillery, in its Anti-Aircraft Division. What a let-down! Instead of flying airplanes, I was to shoot them down. Accordingly, I was shipped (notice the service word "shipped" like a bag of wheat, instead of "transported") to Ft. Eustis, Virginia (located in Lee Hall, Virginia), for basic training (I think I got to go into that small town once during my stay, and it must not have been memorable, for I do not recall much of anything from that visit — do you suppose I was too young?).

The Anti-Aircraft Division was so proud of its new technology, two giant megaphone ears about eight or ten feet apart used to determine which direction the planes were coming from, and manipulated with electric motors.

I was just completing basic coastal artillery training, when I was very grudgingly advised that I was being reassigned to the Army Air Corps. The other branches were extremely jealous of the Army Air Corps, and tended to treat soldiers who were going to that branch with disdain. As a result, I was removed from my group there and assigned to a temporary "pool." During that stay of a month and one-half, I was assigned rather menial (we called them "shitty") duties, such as Kitchen Police (KP), the laundry, yard duty, and all those other "good jobs." My memories of Ft. Eustis, fortunately, are now very vague (as may be surmised, I have no pictures of Ft. Eustis). It is interesting that there is no indication on my discharge papers to the effect that I was ever assigned to the Coastal Artillery prior to going into the Army Air Corps.

Army Air Corps Cadet Basic Training

Finally, again, I received orders to travel. This time we were shipped to Miami Beach — of all places! I found myself on a troop train, in a resurrected coach, along with many, many other soldiers from other areas. The crowded uncomfortable coach was of early vintage, and even had a hole in the floor of the toilet instead of a fixture. We joked about it and said that the train must have hauled Lincoln in his travels during the Civil War. The seats were anything but spotlessly clean. I cannot recall anything about receiving meals. Fortunately, the trip finally ended in Miami, Florida, on 2 June 1943. We were picked up at the late arrival hour of midnight, waiting endlessly to be processed and assigned quarters. We had not had an evening meal, and we had to wait in the huge dining room of the largest hotel on the beach (the Hotel National). The sleepy mess crew served our repast — SOS — creamed beef or "shit on a shingle" as we in the service affectionately called it. I do remember that the meal was not the greatest.

We went to our barracks. I was assigned to the Hotel Biarritz, one of the smallest and the least desirable on the beach, but it was absolute heaven compared to Ft. Eustis. We were crowded into small rooms with steel bunk beds, upper and lower — fortunately I had an upper. Miami Beach seemed like Paradise, with its unique contemporary architecture, its clean streets, its beautiful sandy beach, and its beautiful weather.

We soon learned that the lovely white sandy beach and the wonderful warm weather were actually instruments of torture to us. We performed our physical education on the beach, with a run in the sand before and after other calisthenics. The sun was very hot, and often we would lose a couple of cadets when they passed out. We were not allowed to assist them. They had to just stay where they fell, until they recovered. If we had to march, we had to step over them, in cadence, of course. This basic training was intended to weed out anyone whom the Army Air Corps felt was not suited to becoming a flying officer. There were also other ways of weeding out people. One was if a cadet received a sunburn so severe that he had to go on sick call (note the use of the masculine pronoun here and subsequently, for there were very, very few

Aviation Cadet Vaughn at Hotel Biarritz, Miami Beach, Florida, "barracks" for Army Air Corps Basic Training.

female personnel in our experience in the Army Air Corps at that time). I got a sunburn one weekend, but it was not severe enough for sick call, fortunately. Drill practice was in full uniform, including a Springfield rifle, on the hot streets of Miami Beach ("parade rest" was a most welcome sound).

On weekends we would go to the USO, which was located on the beach and "manned" by very friendly and helpful "older" ladies. The USO served meals, for a fee, and the food was a glorious change from our regular fare. Two desserts I especially enjoyed were key-lime pie and fresh coconut pie. They would literally have someone climb a tree, pick coconuts, shuck them, and make the pie while we were there (isn't it strange the things one remembers and the things one forgets?). One of our greatest entertainments was to visit the numerous stands around the beach which served fresh orange juice squeezed in front of our eyes. Those stands had another appeal, for there one saw practically the only "younger" girls in the area.

College Training Detachment

The next stop after Miami Beach was Springfield College in Massachusetts

Springfield College, Massachusetts, College Training Detachment (pre-World War II postcard).

Mrs. Pendleton, Head Hostess of the Springfield USO, her father, and Aviation Cadet Vaughn.

(the birthplace of basketball) for College Training Detachment. We were there for two months, and this was an attempt to fill in the gaps in our formal college education, with regular college courses and plenty of drill and athletics. We had the Cadet class system there with "square meals" (awkwardly moving food from the plate to the mouth in 90° movements), gigs (double-time marches around the perimeter of the area), and all those good things. I really enjoyed my stay there and made many good friends.

The USO in Springfield (I think it was in the Art Gallery) was a great place for us where we went to dances and other events. It was there I met Mrs. Pendleton who took us Springfield College Cadets under her wing. She helped us get through some rough times. In a 28 February 1944 letter from her she said, the USO was "going strong. We had a large crowd last night."

At one time, practically everyone in the college became ill from ptomaine poisoning. I recovered quickly, but before I was fully recuperated, I was placed on guard duty, and struggled throughout the night. On the brighter side, we had seven hours of flight time in a Piper Cub while there. It practically flew itself, so it was no great challenge, except it really didn't want to land. It was just enough to whet our appetites for "the real thing."

Actually, the life at Springfield College was so good that a group of us wanted to stay, but that was not to be. There were six of us who came from Miami, who had been friends there. We operated as a group and were called "The Miami Six." I wrote about the group in my diary.

> Metrinko, Miner, Moore, Murphy, Massey and Vaughn (how I ever got in with this unholy bunch is beyond me since I was at the end of the alphabet) composed this odd aggregation. We first noticed the strangeness (which later proved to be humorous and the image of the fellows): Metrinko — he was a Wall Streeter, was in Pearl Harbor when it was bombed, always wore sun glasses; Miner was a Sergeant from Cleveland and married to a nice wife; Moore was a smart looking boy (in dress and mind) from Philadelphia; Massey a tall lanky fellow romantic, zoot sooter, Sinatra-type, from Philadelphia; Murphy was a washed-out Navy cadet (for hedge-hopping), had many ideas and never hesitated to express them, from Texas.
>
> We all left for C.T.D. It was Springfield College. We were greeted with the class system. We gained many friends, because we were the first to come there. We marked a test where we would all get a low score and stay in a lower class. The town was a swell place.
>
> Murphy and I were advanced and shipped to Nashville together. The others came down a month later. Metrinko was washed-out in Nashville. Murphy was made a bombardier (by demand). We both stayed in Nashville another month together. We parted there. . . . What happens to each, only the future can tell.

Classification

All Aviation Cadets in the Eastern Flying Training Command went to Nashville, Tennessee, for testing — psychological, physical, and academic. It was there that the determination was made whether to accept us for further training or wash us out, and where we were assigned for training as pilots, navigators, or bombardiers. I was classified as a pilot, but that joy was muted by having to serve on KP (Kitchen Police) for two Sundays in a row. While in Nashville, I was able to obtain through the Red Cross a farm furlough, to help the family to harvest crops. After returning to Nashville, I had time to do some painting. One of my creations depicted a lonely pine tree in a pastoral scene. It was painted on fiber wallboard, with enamels. I still have the painting, but it has suffered from the shrinking of the wallboard and from tropical termites in St. Croix. This painting, along with others I had done, was viewed by an art collector (I do not recall his name, but he was a civilian, not a soldier), who wanted to buy it from me for his extensive collection of art by military personnel. I was tempted, but refused the offer in the end.

In retrospect, I sometimes wonder how really effective classification and training was. I once knew a bombardier who had acrophobia, a fear of heights. Somehow he not only got through classification but bombardier training. His fear became apparent when we were going to Manila. There was a reconstructed bridge over a river in Manila which had to be crossed. It was planked with landing mats which had holes through them and vibrated when walked on, revealing the swift flowing waters below the bridge. As the bombardier started over the bridge, he looked down, and abruptly stopped. No amount of encouragement, no amount of cajoling, no amount of force could get him to cross over the bridge. He ultimately had to walk miles out of the way to find another bridge over which to pass. He later admitted this fear of heights.

Pre-Flight Training

Maxwell Field, Alabama, was the scene for pre-flight training. We studied military customs, went to classes, and even went through the experience of the pressure chamber. It was there that I was a "volunteer" to take my oxygen mask off at 38,000 feet. I didn't last long before becoming unconscious. We were to write our name over and over, but I got only one and one-half completed. A number of people got the bends, as I did one time, but it disappeared ultimately after slow depressurization.

We often had to stand in the pouring rain at parade rest waiting to get into the dining room, as well as in parades, and other occasions. Shortly after I celebrated my 19th birthday at Maxwell I went to the hospital because of pneumonia. I had to wait for a bed while sitting in the hall with a 104° fever for half a day. While there, the nurses made a mistake and stuck cotton swab sticks up into my sinuses, instead of the person in the next bed. That caused me some additional infection which I did not have before. I recovered quickly, however, and went back to my duties.

Primary Flight Training

On 12 February 1944 we were finally assigned to our primary flight training base, Darr Aero Tech in Albany, Georgia. Our first real flying was to begin with the old reliable PT-13 Stearman (also known as the Boeing Kaydet). My 1 March 1944 diary entry illustrates the problems in attempting to learn to fly.

Today, I shot landings all period. I now have six hours and thirty-eight minutes. In the next ride [after flying with me], my instructor and his student ran into a marker and broke 3 ribs [whose, I don't

Aviation Cadet Vaughn, Maxwell Field Pre-Flight School Class of 44-H. (Photo by Joseph Vaughn)

Barracks, Darr Aero Tech Primary Flight Training School, Albany, Georgia.

Boeing Stearman PT-13.

Aviation Cadet Vaughn in Primary Flight Training flying attire.

recall]. They have to report to the Safety Board tomorrow and I imagine there won't be much flying for us.

Every pilot remembers his first solo flight. Mine was memorable, at least to me, for in my diary, on 9 March 1944, this is how it happened:

I soloed today for the first time. . . . I [had] made three landings and . . . my instructor, just before he got out said, "This time I'm not

Aviation Cadet Vaughn's crew on the flight line, Darr Aero Tech, Albany, Georgia.

Aviation Cadet Vaughn's crew at the planes on the flight line.

Ernest W. Lindburg, Vaughn's instructor, Darr Aero Tech, Albany, Georgia.

going to tell you a thing today because — I'm not going to be here with you.

Not all went well all the time with my flight training. We all had our problems. I believe part of mine was because I was concerned when my brother Jim was shot down in Europe on the 22 February 1944 Regensburg, Germany, raid. In spite of those early problems, I eventually graduated with my class of 44-H training (and still have the certificate to prove it.)

Basic Flight Training

Next, it was on to basic flight training on 22 April 1944. This time it was

Aviation Cadet Vaughn with a Boeing PT-13 Stearman Primary Trainer.

Augusta, Georgia. We had BT-13 Vultee Valiant basic trainers, which we affectionately called "Vultee Vibrators." This name resulted from the characteristic of the plane to shudder and vibrate fiercely just before a stall. Most of us liked the plane. A feature which some of us apparently liked was the conveniently placed button for tapping out Morse code. As a result, Cadets with overactive ability would sometimes tap out unspeakable words (at that time). I still remember the codes. Even the honorable SOS was sadly abused, and we were constantly reprimanded for these violations.

During our flight training at Augusta, we Aviation Cadets were treated to a demonstration of an unusual fighter plane, the Bell Aircraft P-39 Airacobra. The small sleek fighter buzzed the field at full throttle, no more than a few feet off the runway. It was a thrilling display of piloting and especially of that fascinating airplane. The pilot and plane seemed to "have the right stuff."

Vultee Valiant BT-13 Basic Flight Trainer. (Courtesy of General Dynamics Corporation)

That event inspired us to work harder and gave us additional incentive to hang on.

Other than the foregoing, my stay at Augusta was rather uneventful. During that time, however, on 6 June 1944, we learned that the invasion of Europe had started, and that Rome had fallen. That did have quite an effect upon everyone. For some unknown reason, unfortunately, I did not have photos of this airbase nor of our BT-13 planes. That is strange, for I really enjoyed my stay there in Augusta.

Advanced Flight Training

Advanced flight training was the final stage from where we would go on to the "real thing." On 29 June 1944 I was assigned to twin-engine training at Moody Field, Valdosta, Georgia, where we flew the AT-10s. The AT-10 was a military version of a Beech aircraft, a general aviation-type plane, adapted for the military.

In all of the flight training, I had no accidents, a constant threat to us and our instructors. The PT-13 Stearman Primary Trainer was a tough airplane, but it was particularly susceptible to being ground-looped because of its narrow wheelbase. We were told if any pilot trainee ground-looped a Stearman and the plane suffered wing damage, the pilot had to pay for it (from the meager $75-a-month pay). I cannot vouch for the fact that Cadets did, in fact, pay for such damage, because I never ground-looped, but I did come close, as did everyone else. Once in basic training I was flying the BT-13 "Vultee Vibrator" during a night flight when I had "vertigo" — actually an optical sensational illusion. It appeared as if two red lights were flying directly at me. I attempted a dodging maneuver and placed the plane into a dive. Reaching the red-line speed (the speed over which it is dangerous to operate the craft), I leveled off and still saw the same two red lights coming at me. They turned out to be the lights on the range beacon towers. It was frightening, and taught me a good lesson, one which I never again violated — don't always trust what you see, but rely more on your instructions from the experts.

In another flight, again I thought I might not only lose the plane, but maybe even the lives of my co-pilot and myself. This was in the AT-10. The weather report was good, visibility good, and we were on a triangular night flight. After we reached our first checkpoint and started on the second leg, the weather socked in totally. We were over halfway into the flight, beyond the point of no return between the first and second checkpoints. We then had no alternative but to continue on the dead reckoning course. It should be added that the radio compass and the radio signals were unusable because of the tremendous amount of lightning, so we had to continue only with dead

Beech AT-10 Advanced Flight Trainer. (Courtesy of Beech Aircraft Corporation)

reckoning (what a term that is). We arrived at the time of our second checkpoint but could not see anything, and again the radio was worthless, so upon expiration of the calculated time, we turned on the final leg. Unknown to us, the wind direction had also changed and had blown us considerably off course. We became rather frantic and instituted fuel conservation measures, for it had become dangerously low. We were temporarily hopelessly lost. Keep in mind that this flying took place around Georgia and Florida over the Okefenokee swamps, not exactly an ideal place to land in an emergency because of snakes and alligators, and remoteness from civilization. Eventually the weather cleared somewhat, so that our range signals and radio compass began to work. We homed into our destination and prayed hard that we would not run out of gas. We were cleared for immediate landing and on the final approach our engines failed. We had already put down full flaps and had opened the cockpit doors and had hung our arms out the openings for drag. This was necessary because we had no hydraulic pressure with our dead-stick landing. We rolled to the end of the runway and finally stopped in the mud. How would you explain that to your instructor?

Graduation — Pilot

I completed my training at Moody and was graduated with Class 44-H on 8 September 1944 as a Flight Officer Twin-Engine Pilot, under the Army Air Forces Eastern Flying Training Command. Again, I did not have my own photos of Moody Field nor of the AT-10. Through the courtesy of Beech Aircraft, however, I was able to obtain a photograph of the AT-10, really a rather handsome aircraft in its day. In my diary I wrote: "D-Day is here. We graduated and pinned on the bars and wings" (blue bars for Flight Officer). I was disappointed that my parents were not able to be in attendance for what I considered the biggest day of my life. They were unable to attend because they were busy harvesting crops before the winter season, and because of labor shortages they could not obtain help to harvest the crops.

Many of us graduate pilots were "commissioned" as Flight Officers (the equivalent of Warrant Officer), whereas others were commissioned as Second Lieutenants. This occurred without any explanation to us as to what method was used to determine how one was classified. Inquiries prior to graduation led us to realize that we had absolutely no influence over which we would receive. It was generally thought that the younger graduates would become Flight Officers and the older ones would become Second Lieutenants, and such was the case for me and my associates.

An article, "The Third Lieutenants," by J. H. MacWilliam and Bruce D. Callander, in *Air Force Magazine* of March 1990 (pp. 100-102), discussed this matter, clearing up some of the Army's silence. That authors called Flight

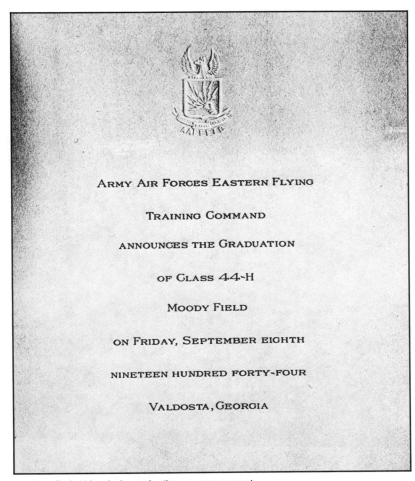

ARMY AIR FORCES EASTERN FLYING

TRAINING COMMAND

ANNOUNCES THE GRADUATION

OF CLASS 44-H

MOODY FIELD

ON FRIDAY, SEPTEMBER EIGHTH

NINETEEN HUNDRED FORTY-FOUR

VALDOSTA, GEORGIA

Aviation Cadet Vaughn's graduation announcement.

Officers "Third Lieutenants" and called their divided blue bars "blue pickles" (the same term we all used at the time).

The military caste system was alive and well in the early 1940s, but it was soon to clash head-on with the realities of rapid mobilization.

The Army Air Corps still required pilot trainees to be at least twenty-one years old and to have at least two years of college, because they were to be commissioned on graduation. . . .

As the pace of the buildup increased, USAAF lowered the entrance requirements for aviation cadets to admit eighteen-year olds with high school diplomas.

Flight Officer Robert V. Vaughn upon graduation from Advanced Flight Training, 8 September 1944.

I responded to that magazine article, in a 17 March 1990 letter indicating the following (published in the *Air Force Magazine*, May 1990):

Perhaps it might be of interest to other readers to hear from another person who graduated as a Flight Officer with a "blue pickle," who served during World War II, and who was proffered a second lieutenancy, after peace was declared. I refused to apply for a second lieutenancy for definite reasons. First of all, if I accepted the commission, I would have to remain in service without enough points to go home, and back to college. . . . In addition most of the second lieutenants with whom I graduated were being offered first lieutenancies. As a result, although we were "more or less" equal as Flight Officers and Second Lieutenants, there would be additional "low man on the totem pole" duties which would gravitate to the new Second Lieutenants.

In the MacWilliam and Callander article, it was indicated that Flight Officers were paid more than Second Lieutenants, $255 per month versus $240 per month. I pointed out in my reply that I did not have to file income tax statements as a Flight Officer but would have to do so as a Second Lieutenant. The final reason was that by accepting a Second Lieutenancy I could be recalled to active duty, like many of my contemporaries who were called to Korea and/or Vietnam.

Just as there was no indication in my discharge that I ever served in the Coastal Artillery, there is no indication that I was ever offered a Second Lieutenancy, nor that I did not accept one. In a 17 October 1945 letter to my parents, I discussed this problem.

I don't believe I told you . . . how the end of the war affected me, did I. I had planned to surprise you and sign my letters with "Lt." instead of "F/O," but things didn't turn out as expected. I was put in for 2nd (Lt.) as soon as I got in the 43rd and I took my physical (64) and all. I was to get my 2nd Lieutenancy and in a couple of months to check out and get 1st (Lt.). But then came the end . . . [for] our commissions.

I did not believe the Army Air Forces would automatically promote from Flight Officer to Second Lieutenant and then, shortly thereafter, to First Lieutenant in as short a time as they verbally indicated they would do.

Concerning officer ranks, one of the crews to which I was reassigned, after undergoing surgery and losing my original crew, consisted of a Major Pilot, a Flight Officer Co-Pilot (me), a Captain Navigator, and a First Lieutenant Bombardier. Well, I can tell you that I, as a Flight Officer, although nominally second in command, was assigned all the duties on that plane, even those which are normally done by other officers. Fortunately, I lost that crew before being shipped overseas, and was assigned to a new crew.

Flight Officer Robert V. Vaughn (top row, l.) with Crew 674 at Charleston Air Base, SC. [Shortly after the picture was taken the author had an emergency appendectomy.]

B-24 Transition Training

After graduation as a Flight Officer pilot, there was further training. B-24 Transition School started on 20 September 1944 at Tyndal Field in Panama City, Florida. While there I had a chance to talk to a Bell Aircraft factory representative and inspect the P-63 Kingcobra fighter. It was a rather large aircraft styled somewhat after the P-39 Airacobra. I was very impressed by the fluid-drive gear train. It adjusted the propeller requirements by increasing or decreasing the fluid in the fluid-drive coupling, a rather novel innovation at that time.

While in the B-24 Transition School, one of the instructors was a hot throttle jockey, if you can imagine that with a B-24. He did a roll with the B-24, and I am certain that it was not built for those stresses. It did, however, leave me with confidence in the plane's structural integrity, but not in the intelligence of the instructor.

Crew and Theater Assignments

We were sent next to Westover Field, Springfield, Massachusetts, on 15 November 1944 for crew assignments, and I met my assigned crew for the first time on 28 November 1944. Charleston, South Carolina, Army Air Base was next, for final checkouts, and for overseas assignment. I was hospitalized there for an appendectomy, and as a result I lost my crew which was shipped to Europe without me. If I had not had appendicitis, I would have gone to Europe instead of Asia. During my stay in Charleston, several times we flew on reconnaissance to try to locate some downed airmen and/or their aircraft. We flew for hours over the Atlantic Ocean to Nassau and into the Bermuda Triangle, an area reputed to be the graveyard of many ships and airplanes. Obviously the military placed credence in it, for we were assigned to fly for hours to the Bermuda Triangle, over it, and back. We saw some flotsam, and reported it, for it looked like a life jacket and part of a bulkhead door.

Somewhere along the line (and I think it was Charleston) we were being taught the intricacies of the new super-secret technologies, including *RADAR*, *LORAN*, and the *Norden Bombsight*. We had no books, and we were not allowed to bring paper and pencils with us to class. We were supposed to remember everything. In retrospect, I rather imagine that the Axis probably knew all about it, though it is amazing how well the landing of troops in Europe was accomplished without the enemy's knowledge.

Later on, we shipped out to Gowen Field in Boise, Idaho, followed by an assignment in Salinas, California. During the final days of flying in the States, our crew came upon a near-disaster. We were flying and following an assigned three-point course which came close to San Francisco. As we approached the city, all of a sudden there were flack bursts all around us. We dived down quickly, and evaded the anti-aircraft fire. It was real, no joke! We later learned that the maps we had been provided had been revised and the area over which we were flying was then restricted. The Navy did its best to down the Army Air Force there. Years later, while participating in a Dale Carnegie Course in Detroit, I gave a talk entitled, "I nearly lost my heart in San Francisco."

Departure from the United States

My final Stateside base was at Hamilton Field near San Francisco, California. While there, I wrote home on 14 July 1945 about those last days:

This is an aerial P.O.E. (Port of Embarkation), a very beautiful post, but these hills are wearing me out. I went to San Francisco a couple of times and had a good time there [I visited the "Top of the Mark" as most people did before going overseas from there]. That town is really hilly. It is really a busy place. The Golden Gate is beautiful as well as awe-inspiring. . . . Spike Jones is supposed to play here tonight with Frances Langford [they did perform for us].

We departed from Hamilton Field in a C-54 Skymaster, similar to the one which General Douglas MacArthur had as his personal plane on Okinawa. There was a full load, and the passengers included a couple of Generals, plus many other high-ranking officers. It was a very long flight, as I recall, about 11 hours. Apparently we had to take a secure course, which included several different headings.

Chapter 3

Foreign Service — Prior to Peace

*May God bless and preserve you and guide you and the Nation
in the effort to ultimate Victory.*

Major General Jonathan M. Wainwright
Letter to President Franklin D. Roosevelt, 5 May 1942

Embarkation

The first landing we made after leaving Hamilton Field, California, was at Hickam Field in Hawaii apparently on 14 July 1945. We stayed in a reinforced concrete barracks where the scars from the strafing by the Japanese was clearly in evidence on the walls. This was a good respite after the long flight, and before taking an even longer trek to our next destination. We were confined to the base, so we did not have an opportunity to visit other areas in Hawaii. Somewhere between 17 July and 23 July 1945 we were enroute again in a C-54. We landed at such strange places as Johnston Island, Midway, Kwajalein Atoll, Guam, Saipan, and Iwo Jima, prior to landing in the Philippines and ultimately in Okinawa, and being transferred to nearby Ie Shima Island. At Kwajalein, in the Flight Room we were greeted, as I recall, by the prophetic humor calligraphed on the walls, something to the effect: "Welcome to Kwajalein Atoll, no fun atall, no booze atall, and no women atall (the latter cleaned up a bit)."

Enroute somewhere between Guam and Clark Field, we altered course to avoid the airspace above the Micronesian island of Yap, which was still under the control of the Japanese, and from which anti-aircraft artillery was capable of downing Allied planes. In a subsequent visit to Iwo Jima, a Marine officer stationed there drove us to the top of Mount Suribachi, where there is a statue

Map of Pacific Theater
1942-1946.

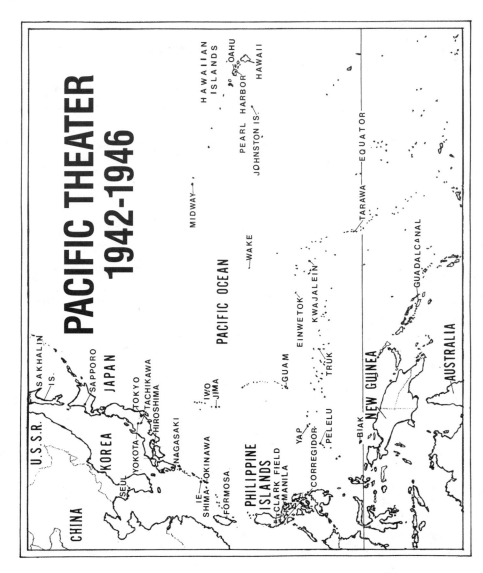

Fifth Air Force shoulder patch.

of the Marines planting the U.S. flag after defeating the Japanese on that island.

Our crew was assigned to the 43rd Bomb Group of the Fifth Air Force. The officers of our crew included Pilot Second Lieutenant Lawrence J. O'Neill, Jr., of Columbus, Ohio; Co-Pilot Flight/Officer Robert V. Vaughn of Carey, Ohio; Navigator Second Lieutenant Fred E. Baker of Sault Ste. Marie, Michigan; and Bombardier Second Lieutenant Jerome Paikin of The Bronx, New York. I might note here that I was assigned to about three different B-24 crews and never had a plane of my own, plus having flown with numerous other pilots in C-46s. As a result I unfortunately never felt really close to my associates. I have never heard from any of my crew members since returning to the United States, nor have I tried to contact them.

My foreign service prior to peace, was spent in primarily two places, Nichols Field in the Philippines and Ie Shima, off the coast of Okinawa. This was during the last days of World War II.

Philippine Islands

Sometime between 17 July and 23 July 1945, I arrived in the Philippines, where we were awaiting assignment and were in a "holding pattern." As such, there were not a lot of duties, as my correspondence with family indicates. Censorship, however, was apparently in full swing, because the words "Rizal Stadium" and "MacArthur" were censored from my letters.

The Filipinos were very friendly. There was, however, a problem with pickpockets in Manila. I lost a new expensive Parker 51 pen, and didn't know it until I got back to camp. In a crowd, a friend of mine lost his GI-issue belt and knew nothing about it either until later (I guess he didn't really need it).

On one excursion there, I traveled into the country, near a stone quarry, where one could still hear the hidden Japanese shooting at soldiers.

In a visit to the only operable cinema, there was a commotion during the show. A Japanese was found hiding in the movie house, where he had been living ever since they had been driven out of Manila. He was badly beaten before he was turned over to the authorities. One movie, by the way, had been showing continuously day and night for months. Its title was *Back to Bataan*. Because the theater never closed, it was really crummy, with stacks of paper boxes and trash under the seats.

The word "gook" first became common in the Philippines. It was the most derogatory generic term used there by the military personnel to indicate Japanese. A less derogatory term used was "Jap."

I mentioned admiration for the Filipino people in a letter of 23 July 1945 to my parents: "A person has to admire these people in a way, for they have lost so much under Japanese hands."

The aforementioned excursion into the countryside was when I was invited to attend a Fiesta with a Filipino boy who did my laundry. In a letter home, 27 July 1945, I indicated the following:

> We had to walk about five miles back in the wilderness where we came to a river. We were pulled across the river in a dugout. It was sort of a ferry. The houses are as one would expect to see in a geographic magazine: little bamboo-thatched roofed homes with little brown children, in their birthday suits, running around. Pigs and chickens are all around. He then took me to his home to meet his family. His father is 36. They have 2 girls and 3 boys and have a very small home with corn growing in the 2-by-4 front yard. The house is a large

bamboo floored room and a kitchen, with a couple of dishes and pans and some rice. For supper they gave me bananas and mangos. . . .

The boy, "Eddie" we call him, who was barefooted before, dressed up in snow white clothes and shoes and took me to the church. It was very large, but not too beautiful. The fiesta was in honor of the patroness of the church and village, St. Anna. She (the image) was placed in a roofed boat (three dugouts lashed together) and was paddled up and down the river. As it went by the houses everyone prayed or the guerrillas shot their guns in her honor. Everyone who had a boat was riding with the image. Naturally the antics of several young fellows were to try to get other people wet. It was a big celebration. Behind the image was a band with Filipino players. They played the Notre Dame Victory song, Pennsylvania Polka and others. Eddie did not have a boat, but got a friend to row us around. The Japanese burned Eddie's boat. Everyone waved and said, "Hello Joe." Everywhere you would walk, people would be glad to see you and say "Cano," meaning "American." The kids would run up and grab your hand and say "Hello Joe." After the boat ride the image was carried in procession through the streets. . . . Everyone kissed the garments. They had a dance afterwards, but I couldn't stay for it because it was dark and I should be getting back. The strange thing is the priest didn't have a thing to do with the procession. He just looked out over it all from the church.

I am invited to another fiesta on the 31st. I hope to go.

One thing I did notice in the countryside in the Philippines was that every home had a sewing machine, usually a "Singer" or a "White."

I did not get many pictures in the Philippines, for I did not have film, although I discovered 127 was available for $2.50; but I indicated in a letter that the film is "not so very good."

Coincidences seem to follow people around. One day while walking down the street in Manila, I heard someone shout my name from across the street. It was a high-school classmate, who graduated with me in a class of about 47 (from a town of about 2,000). I cannot recall his name, would you believe. I recall another event where I encountered another person, Corrine Krupp, from our small town of Carey, Ohio.

In the Philippines, we did not have to worry much about Japanese air attacks. The only problem was once in a while an individual Japanese would attack someone for food and money, and skitter into the bush. The camps in the Philippines were very uncomfortable, especially during the rainy season. At one time, our camp became a sea of mud. The water would gush through our tents, causing the cot legs to sink, lowering the canvas into the mud itself. To top it all off, the rain eventually came through the tent fabric. Then, to make matters worse, came the scourge of millions of mosquitoes, with nothing to keep them off except the mosquito bars — the nets, which only increased the temperature and humidity, making sleep practically impossible.

I wrote home about going dancing, indicating that I had an enjoyable time. The dances were somewhat more primitive than what I had been accustomed to, because of the lack of facilities. I went dancing in town two times. During these escapades, we drank the local rum in brown beer bottles. It was potent. During one of these adventures, I bumped into a pilot of a P-38, and we became friends. During the course of the evening, he said he would like to fly a bomber, and I said I would like to fly a fighter. We, then, agreed to swap jobs and fly each other's plane — we had never given a thought to the fact that neither had been checked out in the aircraft. Fortunately, the next day, I forgot about it and so did he.

On one of my flights over the Philippines, I took photos of Corregidor Island in the entrance of Manila Bay, near the Bataan Peninsula, Luzon. That island was invaded in May 1942 by the Japanese and was returned in March 1945.

Eventually, this stint in the Philippines came to an end, and we were transferred.

Ie Shima

Somewhere between 1 August and 12 August 1945, we and our B-24s arrived on Ie Shima, a very small island, with one hill, an airbase, and beautiful sand beaches, with little vegetation. The island is just off the coast of Okinawa, which could be easily seen from our airbase. This island was badly bombed during the invasion, and little is left. Ernie Pyle, the noted journalist, was killed there. Upon arrival, we were greeted on radio (from Japan) by the sweet American-accented voice of Tokyo Rose. I wrote to my parents about it on 30 August 1945 *after the war*.

The paper [*Stars and Stripes*] says they found Tokyo Rose who is an American citizen. I heard her several times and when the 43rd Bomb Group came over here, she greeted us. After most [of us] arrived, and when we [the U.S.] gave the Japanese an ultimatum, Tokyo Rose gave us 24 hours to get off the island or she would rub us off the map [she threatened to use poison gas]. Of course we laughed at her, and we also prepared for her. We were issued gas masks and accessories and ammo.

Ie Shima Island, off the coast of Okinawa.

Ie Shima was similar to a "land-based aircraft carrier," for it was so small that the airstrip extended almost from one side to the other. Landing on the strip was not the easiest thing, for we had to fly in directly over a sheer cliff. There were many types of aircraft located on Ie Shima. I rather imagine that it was done for safety, for Okinawa, the nearby large island, was within sight, heavily defended, and had a great number of aircraft located there also. It became apparent that these aircraft were being assembled for the final bombing and invasion of Japan.

I was able to go to Okinawa, where I saw the huge B-32. It was apparently a prototype or "sister-type" of the B-29, with the appearance resembling a B-24. There were not many of those planes, perhaps five or six. Later on, we were to conjecture that they were there in case the B-29s did not work out, and perhaps to confuse the Japanese in case they had to be used for the atomic bomb. I took some photos of Ie Shima from the air, but the negatives were not very good.

While on Okinawa, we visited a beach near General MacArthur's headquarters. The beaches around Okinawa and Ie Shima were beautiful.

Life on Ie Shima was not all fun and games. We had makeshift tents, and a makeshift "mess," which doubled as the "Officers' Club" (where the

Flight Officer Elmo Curtis beside a B-32 bomber at Yontan, Okinawa.

specialty was "Rum and Coke," with the rum coming from the Philippines in the old beer bottles). We did most of the construction of our own tents and dug our own foxholes nearby. In a letter home 7 September 1945, while not identifying the location, I discussed our building efforts: "Today we started building our home. We got half of the floor built for our tent, and we got in

Flight Officer Vaughn in front of a B-32 at Yontan, Okinawa.

electricity today. It certainly is a luxury after so long."

Almost all of us pitched in to build the raised wooden floor, and to erect the tent over it. Would you believe, as we were nearing completion, the one officer on our crew who did practically nothing in the building, got his camera.

Okinawa beach scene near General MacArthur's headquarters.

General Douglas MacArthur's C-54 airplane on Okinawa.

Flight Officer Vaughn beside a P-38 Lightning fighter.

picked up a hammer, held it up, posed, and said, "Take my picture building our house." Oh well. . . .

There is an old Army phrase, "when in the field improvise." Well, there was a new twist on Ie Shima, for one enlisted man and his crew built their home, but also dug a "basement." There was a concealed door in the floor under a footlocker. The area was just large enough for their equipment, a metal drum with which they were going into the production of wine. They "midnight requisitioned" sugar, raisins, prunes, and other dried fruit from the Mess Hall. These were placed in the drum and then filled with water, and allowed to ferment. All was going OK, with the conglomeration becoming more and more potent, along with the smell. They finally got to drink some of the stuff (I do not know how you could honestly call it wine), along with some headaches. Their entrepreneurship came to an abrupt halt, however, when their "home" was unexpectedly inspected because of reports of a strange odor. There were reprimands for all, and that was the end of the wine misadventure.

At first we thought the food was good, but soon it became apparent that they were running out of fresh food, for rather consistently we started having canned mutton stew from Australia and New Zealand. It was particularly obnoxious because of its smell, but, in addition, it was greasy, and if the stew became cold, the grease would form on our metal utensils. Fresh food was rare.

Air Attacks

During the time we spent on Ie Shima, we encountered nightly air attacks from the Japanese. These were timed to interrupt our normal sleep; however, because of the fact that they became a regular occurrence, we were able to adjust our sleep habits. Under these attacks we jumped into our foxholes and were glad we had them. During some attacks, the twin-engine radar-controlled Northrop P-61 Black Widow night fighters from our base would attempt to down the Japanese planes, but this was only done when visibility permitted and when the 90-mm anti-aircraft batteries (AAA) were not defending our base. On many occasions bombs would be dropped on our planes, and we lost a number, including P-38s, B-24s, and C-46s, etc. The attacks were nerve-wracking, for if the Black Widows were used, the dogfight sounds were horrendous. The use of AAA guns, however, was almost of greater concern to us than the bombs the Japanese were dropping (our quarters were a considerable distance from the flight line) because the artillery pieces were in our "back yard" so to speak. As such, the unbelievable sound of the 90-mm guns being fired resounded in our ears, and actually almost deafened us for a short time. In addition, there was the eerie flash from the artillery

Northrop P-61 Black Widow Night Fighter, radar equipped. (Courtesy of Northrop Corporation)

being discharged. The greatest concern, however, was that because of the proximity of the AAA pieces, the shrapnel would fall all about, hitting the corrugated steel roofs of our mess hall, and landing on our tents. There was the potential for setting them on fire. The shrapnel would also fall on us in our foxholes, for it usually came down vertically. Usually no one was injured seriously from the shrapnel, as I recall (more bark than bite, I guess).

While on Ie Shima, we experienced a serious typhoon which destroyed most of our tent "homes," our mess hall/officers club, and, most serious, the walls on our latrine. The latrine was the usual pit-type construction, located upon a hillock downwind from our camp. All that remained after the typhoon was the bench with the holes cut in it. I recall how strange it seemed to see someone sitting way up there silhouetted against the full moon on a clear night. It was a little more troublesome when the rains came and the mosquitoes followed.

Bombing Missions

During our stint on Ie Shima, it appeared that the U.S. Navy was a problem

The B-24 "All American" in flight. (Courtesy of General Dynamics Corporation)

B-24s in formation on a raid to Japan.

to us. At the end of the war, they were trying to gain credit for doing so many things. Apparently this was so that they would have larger budgets in the future. There appeared to be little or no communication between the Navy and the Army, except in the area of the rescue of downed fliers. All too often this lack of communication resulted in our planes going on a mission, only to have the Navy beat us to it that day. This might not really have been that bad, but when the primary target was gone, we proceeded to the alternate target. Sometimes we would find that it, too, was already taken. Again, this might not have been so bad, but there was a steel strike in the U.S. during the war. As a result, there was a shortage of bombs, and each one had to be used judiciously. This meant that if your primary and alternate targets were gone you had to return carrying those bombs, perhaps partially armed with proximity detonating devices. On one such trip, a bomb was found to have its safety pin missing. Because of the extra weight, the plane had to be landed on Ie Shima at a higher speed on the postage-stamp-sized strip, while making certain that the altitude was greater than the cliff at the end of the runway. Pilot skill was crucial at those times, especially when the weather was not ideal.

A crew beside a B-24 identical to the number and make-up of crew members and planes flown by Flight Officer Vaughn.

Atomic Bomb

Much of the foregoing was not previously written down or recorded, for we were not really permitted to maintain diaries, nor generally to take photographs. What was not often written down was that there was a rumor that the United States was going to drop a "super bomb" on Japan (note that in those days the word "super" had a much stronger connotation than it does today — it compared to or was stronger than the modern young people's word "humungus."). It was then that we surmised that the B-32s on Okinawa were to be used in case the B-29s did not prove successful. On a bombing raid to Japan several days after the bombing of Hiroshima, we flew low over Hiroshima (although we were told *not* to do so but were *not* really told about radiation); I took some photographs (even though we were told not to bring cameras along, much less take photographs). I have always suspected that some of the spots on the photographs, and part of the poor delineation were due to the radiation. It was, in the modern vernacular, "awesome." It was like a huge brown oval surrounded by green hills away from the blast area. A visit a couple of days later to Nagasaki was also as awesome, although the destruction did not appear to me to be as extensive as at Hiroshima.

After the end of the war on 31 October 1945, I wrote to my family about the atomic bomb and other Japanese military matters.

> I noticed in the *Stars and Stripes* that 106 out of 145 Japanese warships are still in good commission and the Americans thought they were almost completely out. I could have told anyone that for I saw the complete Japanese Navy lined up in a harbor *before* the peace was declared. I had never seen so many ships. There were [on a bombing mission] battleships, cruisers, destroyers, and two aircraft carriers all aligned up in a perfect line, however we were not allowed to bomb any ships. We had to hit the primary or secondary target *only*. I saw the places which the two A-Bombs hit — rather brown and deserted.
>
> It was rumored here about them, long before it was released. Everyone couldn't believe it but had the highest hopes for the end of the war.

The dropping of that super bomb was preceded, on Ie Shima, by the United States preparing for an invasion of Japan, in case the bomb did not work, or in case the Japanese refused to surrender. In preparation, we had carpenters rapidly installing wooden benches inside the bomb bays of the B-24s. More and more planes and troops were being landed on Ie Shima. We were not happy with the thought of trying to land these cumbersome overloaded less-than-agile planes in a hostile, highly defended area. There is no doubt in my

Atomic bomb devastation at Hiroshima, Japan, taken by Flight Officer Vaughn a few days after the bomb was dropped (from the window of a B-24 on a raid to Japan).

mind that such an invasion would have failed, or at least prolonged the surrender for years (if the atomic bombs had not been effective). This was reinforced when we finally landed in Japan after the war, after seeing all the pillboxes on many street corners, and after having seen manufacturing equipment alongside the roads in mountain tunnels, and the many troops still remaining in Japan.

Another view of bomb devastation at Hiroshima.

In William Craig's *The Fall of Japan* (New York, 1967, p. 42), he indicates that the Japanese were preparing an all-out defense of Japan, called *Ketsu-Go*, in case of an Allied invasion. That, of course, reinforces my opinion about the difficulty of invading Japan, and obliquely the partial justification for the use of the atomic bomb.

It was at this time that I became convinced that not only was the dropping of the atomic bomb justified, but that it ended the war without additional bloodshed and misery throughout Japan (and the rest of the world). It also served as a warning that the dropping of other atomic bombs in other wars was not an acceptable alternative. Along with that, it also subsequently became a warning that the much more powerful nuclear bombs could not be used.

It is my contention that the demonstration that *205,000* persons could be annihilated by the dropping of *only two* atomic bombs actually saved the lives of perhaps *9,000,000* or *10,000,000* people in Japan. It also showed to the world that the atomic bomb (and the enormously more powerful nuclear bombs) could *not* be used as a viable offensive war weapon. Can you imagine

A different view of bomb devastation at Hiroshima.

what would have happened if such a bomb were dropped in the Arab-Israeli conflict, in Lebanon, or in the "Desert Storm" Gulf war of 1991? That *might* have happened if we had not had a demonstration of the enormous destructive capability of atomic (and nuclear) bombs.

After the end of the war on 14 October 1945, I wrote to my family from Yokota, Japan, about Japanese aircraft, including the Kamikaze, and about the possibility of invasion.

There are a lot of Kami-Kazi airplanes here. They are very sleek looking jobs. You know the Japanese have sort of a twin engine superfort, pressurized chamber, etc. It is supposed to be able to stay up for 52 hours. It was planned for attacks on U.S. They really have some fine equipment, in fact their workmanship far exceeds some of U.S. work. It was not particularly inferiority of equipment that defeated them, but not enough equipment. Had they not surrendered, an invasion would have been impossible for they have lookouts all over, cave systems, etc. It would have been a terrible defeat (as far as loss of life is concerned for U.S.) even though we could have won.

When one examines the terrain of the two atomic bomb sites of Hiroshima (1970 population, 541,834) and Nagasaki (1970 population, 421,055), one can see that the United States spared many more people from more severe destruction in surrounding areas and in more heavily populated areas. Tokyo in 1973 had a population of 8,583,000, whereas Yokohama had 2,279,483 in 1971, plus the other surrounding population centers. Over 130,000 persons were killed or injured in the Hiroshima strike on 5 August 1945, and 90 percent of the city, located in a valley facing the inland sea, was leveled. From the air one could see that the bomb blast covered an enormous brown egg-shaped area, and it was confined between the hills surrounding Hiroshima. If that same bomb had been dropped on Tokyo, the loss of life would have been enormous, and the city would have been stunted for development in the future. It is somewhat curious as to why Hiroshima was selected for the first drop of an atomic bomb, for the area was not on the first landfall, and the aircraft had to fly over considerable land (probably much highly fortified) before reaching the target. Nagasaki, which was the first port to see Western trade, on the other hand, is located on the south coast of the southernmost Japanese main island of Kyushu, almost facing the open sea. The second atomic bomb was dropped there on 9 August 1945 (four days after the bombing of Hiroshima), killing or wounding about 75,000 people.

In a letter to the Editor of the *Miami Herald*, 3 January 1973, a reader named Audrey Tanner stated, under the headline, "One Man's Courage Ended World War II":

Re your Dec. 28 [1972] editorial in Herald, I couldn't agree with you less. Give 'em hell and lots of it.

We could still be fighting the Japanese if one man had not had the courage to drop an atomic bomb. Thank God for him.

World opinion? People won't like us? So What? I have spent the past four years traveling the world and I can vouch for it — we are very little liked. But we are admired up to the eyebrows and envied in the same ratio. That's human nature.

Much speculation has been made concerning the legitimacy of dropping the *second* atomic bomb, particularly by American troops in the area, who were the most deeply affected Americans at the time, because of its effects on their lives. In my mind, no one should really have been surprised that we dropped the second bomb. It was the general consensus among us airmen that the second atomic bomb had to be dropped because the Japanese officials who were working towards surrender were not at all convinced that the United States had more bombs. As such, the Americans had little choice but to demonstrate to the Japanese that we had more than the first one. It was to cinch surrender that the second atomic bomb was dropped.

In addition to the foregoing, there was the thought of a "Russian threat," that they might at the last minute declare war on Japan and attempt to occupy Japanese territory (as they ultimately did in the southern part of Sakhalin Island). Can anyone imagine what Japan would have been like today, or how many problems would still exist for Japan and the Allied forces with divided Japanese occupation areas? Can anyone also imagine carving up Tokyo and creating another "Berlin Wall?"

Paper Bombs

Actually, the Japanese were forewarned about the possibility of our using "super bombs." Prior to the dropping of the atomic bombs and all kinds of other bombs, B-29s were used to drop "paper bombs" on Japan — forewarnings in the form of pamphlets or leaflets. Apparently at least four pieces of propaganda pamphlets were dropped. I was aware of three, but John Toland, in *The Rising Sun* (New York, 1970, p. 799), alludes to one which I have not seen (nor discovered in reading), resulting in a total of four. The first one Toland discusses indicates that the first 16 million pamphlets were very poor and ineffective because of inept and archaic transliterations and incorrect illustration. I do not know the date of that pamphlet, but it probably was dropped sometime between 16 July and 5 August 1945.

The second pamphlet, mentioned by Toland was apparently dropped prior to 8 August 1945 and contained the following message:

TO THE JAPANESE PEOPLE
America asks that you take immediate heed of what we say on this leaflet.
We are in possession of the most destructive explosive ever devised by man. A single one of our newly developed atomic bombs is

actually the equivalent in explosive power to what 2,000 of our giant B-29s can carry on a single mission. This awful fact is one for you to ponder and we solemnly assure you that it is grimly accurate.

We have just begun to use this weapon against your homeland. If you still have any doubt, make inquiry as to what happened to Hiroshima when just one atomic bomb fell on that city.

Before using this bomb to destroy every resource of the military by which they are prolonging this useless war, we ask that you now petition the Emperor to end the war. Our President has outlined for you the thirteen consequences of an honorable surrender. We urge that you accept these consequences and begin work of building a new, better and peace-loving Japan.

You should take these steps now to cease military resistance. Otherwise, we shall resolutely employ this bomb and all our other superior weapons to promptly and forcefully end the war.

Evacuate your cities now!

While in Japan after the war, Papa Tsugumo, my Japanese host "father," gave me a leaflet which was picked up after it was dropped on Tokyo by an American B-29. I do not know when it was dropped, but it must have been after the first pamphlet and before the second and third mentioned by Toland. This might be assumed because there is no mention of Hiroshima or Nagasaki in the leaflet given to me. It was postcard-sized, printed on both sides on relatively heavy paper — not card stock paper (it appeared to be "reconstituted" paper), in green and black ink. A friend of mine on St. Croix, Virgin Islands, Motakazu Tsu Tsui, translated it for me in 1969. This must have been the actual second "paper bomb."

> The Japanese Staff concerned with military strategy were proud in stating that the defense of Japan is like an iron curtain, which keeps everyone out. They also stated that if anyone tried to attack Japan, the Navy and Air Force could destroy all of them.
>
> However, new America is not only able to attack Japan freely and easily but also can attack daily. The Japanese Staff has no power to avoid these attacks. The Japanese Air Force and Navy are even unable to perform their responsibilities of defense.
>
> The Japanese Staff's stating that Japan could not be attacked does not make any sense. This means that they cannot be trusted to conduct the defense of Japan.
>
> The main American offensive against Japan has not really started yet. When it does start, everybody and everything in Japan will be destroyed.

Propaganda leaflet dropped by American B-29s over Tokyo presented to Flight Officer Vaughn by Papa Tsugumo.

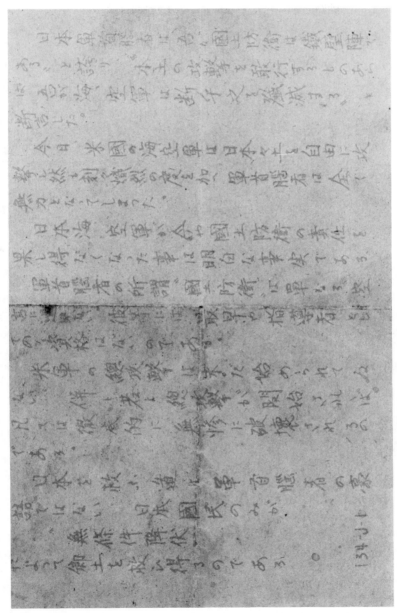

Text side (reverse) of the propaganda leaflet dropped over Tokyo.

The way to save Japan is not with the Staff's big mouths, but by the Japanese people surrendering unconditionally.

The other leaflet mentioned by Toland was obviously dropped *after* Hiroshima *and* Nagasaki. Toland indicates that it was dropped on Tokyo by a single B-29 on 14 August 1945. It contained this message.

TO THE JAPANESE PEOPLE

These American planes are not dropping bombs on you today. They are dropping leaflets instead because the Japanese Government has offered to surrender, and every Japanese has a right to know the terms of that offer and the reply made to it by the United States Government on behalf of itself, the British, the Chinese, and the Russians. Your government now has a chance to end the war immediately.

Surrender

On 19 August 1945 the Japanese surrender team landed on the island of Ie Shima at around 2:00 that afternoon. We knew they were coming, and although we were warned that there was a possibility of some sort of Kamikaze effort, we were authorized to assemble for their arrival. It was hot and blindingly bright on that coral runway. What a sight it was to see the two Japanese "Betty" bombers slowly approaching with an escort of American P-38s and apparently B-25s. I took photographs along with hundreds of other soldiers. It became apparent that the tall, six-foot-plus, American officers chosen to meet and escort the Japanese officials were selected to tower over the much smaller Japanese. The Japanese were in full military uniform and were carrying flowers. The Japanese officer, General Kawabe as I recall, led his contingent to the awaiting C-54 transport. Extremely little time was spent on the ground on Ie Shima. On 21 August 1945, I wrote to my family about the incident:

Well, the news I could send you would be old to you now, for no doubt you heard it, or read it in the papers. Yes, I am and have been on Ie Shima (the site of the first landing of the Japanese surrender party). I went to see the landing on the first date, and they didn't come in. The second time I was there. It was a grand sight to see the two Japanese Bettys and their escorts, P-38s. I took a few pictures. It is strange that there was such a poor paint job on these airplanes, and the green paint (green crosses painted on the planes) was more black than green. The place was really guarded for their safety, but everyone was there more out of curiosity than arrogance. There were no demonstrations at all.

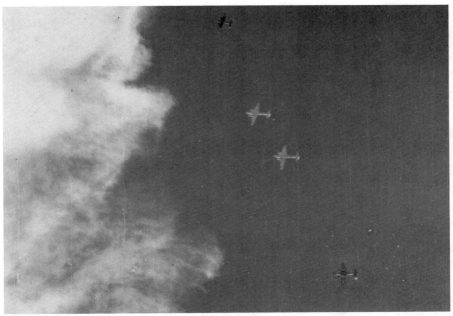

Japanese surrender planes, "Bettys," being escorted over Ie Shima Island off the coast of Okinawa, the first American-held area where the Japanese surrender party landed.

They were dressed in very fine clothes, but the ships seemed to be in very poor condition. [Actually one of the planes on its return to Japan had to ditch in the ocean near a beach in Japan, so my observations were very accurate.] Well, the news all seems very good doesn't it? No doubt there will be a long stay for us new men over here.

The actual surrender of the Japanese was not consummated on Ie Shima, but instead in Tokyo Bay. V-J Day was celebrated on 3 September 1945 on Ie Shima with memorial services at the cemetery with its "symmetrical rows of GI white crosses." They held a high Mass, and as I was standing there I looked down and saw the name "T/4 H. W. Vaughn" — no relation, but a haunting irony.

On V-J Day there was cause for celebration, and celebrations usually call for toasts, which call for "spirits." There were almost no spirits (liquor) around on V-J Day. However, in anticipation of this day, I had made advanced provision. I had an AC/DC portable radio, which in those days was more like an overnighter suitcase. I knew that the huge batteries it required would not last, so when leaving the U.S. there was no purpose in adding their weight to the already heavy radio. I had located two square glass bottles which were

A Japanese surrender plane landing on Ie Shima.

One of the Japanese surrender planes taxiing on Ie Shima.

Some of the Japanese surrender party disembarking a "Betty" airplane on Ie Shima.

identical in size to the batteries. I filled them with Seagram's 7 whiskey. As a result, when V-J Day came, I could offer a "respectable" toast and cheers. My associates appreciated my advanced planning (they had not known about its presence, or we probably would not have toasted V-J Day).

At one time during my stay on Ie Shima, I constructed a hand-guided, gas-engine model airplane from a kit. One of the precious nonmilitary items I had brought from the States was that model kit and engine. I worked hard and long on the model, and when it was finished, I was afraid to fly it, for it meant so much to me, and was really beautiful. As a result, I sold the completed model to someone outside our outfit. I heard later that the person wrecked it. I wrote my family on 12 August 1945 about the completion of that model:

> I had a little time today, so I worked on my airplane [model]. It is a big job, but little by little I will get it completed. The model is a very sleek looking job, and is supposed to go 90 miles an hour. That is much faster than I hope it will go. It is a control-line cable job. It is supposed to be able to do stunts. I have a class B engine of about ⅕th horsepower. I had it operating at one of last bases and it really revs up.

Later, in a letter of 24 August, I discussed the completion of the model, and I should add that I did not get a photograph of the finished model:

> Well, I have my model airplane almost finished. I painted it an odd

A Japanese surrender party in the shade of the C-54 airplane used to fly them to Manila.

A Japanese surrender party boarding the C-54 airplane for the flight to Manila.

color, but had to utilize what dope I could lay my hands on. I want to take a picture of it. I hope it flies ok.

Air Cargo Transport

About a month later our future was being determined, a future which will be discussed in detail in the subsequent chapter. I wrote to my family on 22 September 1945:

> Our outfit is being broken up . . . probably to C-46s or C-47s. I am going to Cargo Transport. . . . We will probably be located in the Southern Philippines. . . . I hate to lose everyone I know, but if I get into transports, I think I will be happy. That is if they don't stick us back in some jungle and run milk runs.

My actual destination assignment was obscured, for again I wrote to my family on 1 October 1945:

> This will probably be my last letter from "Ie" for I am being shipped out today as I had previously told you. Latest rumors are

Southern Luzon. O'Neill left today for Manila. He is going to Troop Transport Command.

It seems the entire outfit fell apart. So many have already left (few, and very few, for the States) and many more soon. It burns everyone up here for they say the 43rd B [bomb] Group is going home and then they transfer us out of it and take in a lot of strangers.

Somewhere between the date when that letter was written on 1 October and the next letter on 8 October 1945, I wrote that I was being shipped to Japan. It would appear that the date was either 4 or 5 October. Thus began my occupation duty stint in Japan.

Chapter 4

Japan — Occupation Service

A time to love, a time to hate;
a time of war, and a time of peace.

Ecclesiastics 3:8

Occupation Duty

At first, occupation duty was a time of military administrative confusion, which was not generally known outside of those military personnel involved. It did, however, have a significant effect upon the occupation duties of military personnel assigned to Japan. With a change from total war to total peace overnight, accompanied by the change in authority from the enemy to the occupation personnel, and changes in all levels of military personnel, there would be confusion. The very record-keeping of personnel was a problem which prevented knowing *who* was there, *where* they were, and *what* they were doing. For example, the military lost my personal medical records in Ie Shima, prior to our departure for Japan. As a result, it was necessary to take all the inoculations again. After the fourth consecutive injection I passed out, but still had to undergo the balance on another day.

Because of the confusion, there was really almost nothing for us to do except fly when requested. There were almost no ground duties during the first stage of occupation, although later on I was placed in charge of the Officers Club. With no ground duties to speak of and very little flying to be done, there was almost nothing to do on base. As a result, there was time to explore Japan. The only limitations were distance from the base and the duty to report in daily. While we loved the flying, we did not particularly appreciate the absolute boredom experienced.

The Yokota Army Air Base, Reno Tower, Fussa, Japan, with a Kamikaze plane on "guard."

It would appear that we were in Japan for one of two contingencies (besides the obvious need to assist in air transportation) — to be available in case of uprisings in Japan itself or offensive intrusion by the Russians (this name was used rather than USSR).

Yokota

My postwar occupation duty began with assignment to the 2nd Combat Cargo Group at Yokota Army Air Base (Reno tower) in Japan, near a small village called Fussa. Our flight to Japan was on 2 October 1945 (five days after the first occupation forces under Colonel Charles T. Tench left Okinawa with the first troops, which landed in Japan). My account of that event was recorded in my monograph, *An American Airman's Experiences in Post-War Japan (1945-1946)*:

> We were picked up in a Curtiss Commando (C-46) that belonged to the outfit to which we were being transferred, namely the Second Combat Cargo Group. Upon leaving Ie Shima . . . we found that we were to fly to a little airfield in Honshu, named Yokota. After traveling over an undercast for a few hours, we let down through the turbulent air and found a small bay and an airfield nearby. The name of the airfield was told to me, but as the Japanese names were new to me, I forgot the name immediately [in retrospect, I think it was Atsugi on Honshu]. There were a few Japanese airplanes in neglected condition scattered throughout the area. The landing strip was small, but the "46" had no difficulty in landing there. We all got out and stretched our weary limbs, while the ship was being refueled.
>
> After the refueling was completed, we took off and the time seemed to fly swiftly by, now that we were nearing our destination. This trip afforded us a better chance to see the destruction in Japan. Evidently the reporters had not exaggerated the story. On landing at

A Kamikaze plane at Yokota.

Yokota, we were greeted by the little men, who obligingly removed our luggage and delivered it to our respective squadrons.

Our ride through the camp to our squadron area gave us a chance to observe how neatly the Japanese had decorated parts of the camp. Their love of nature was apparent by the little gardens and shrines throughout the camp.

Under Japanese control, Yokota was a small air base apparently used for testing experimental aircraft, which were developed in nearby Tachikawa. There were many experimental airplanes on the ground. Later we noted that the Navy had arrived shortly after our arrival and had collected a great many of these experimental planes. That collecting eventually stopped after the Army had established itself. I recall one plane in particular, a twin-engine low-wing small, sleek craft, which appeared to me to have been developed for reconnaissance. There was no known designation for this aircraft. The distinct feature of the plane was its extremely large engine exhausts exiting directly from the middle of the rear of the nacelle. That may not have been a great nor original innovation, but what else it did have was sensational. Just behind the engine exhausts, extending from a rod through the exhaust, were metal spheres which appeared to be made of stainless steel. Apparently this was a form of supercharging. Instead of using the engine exhaust to drive a supercharger to force air into the intake, this system created a Bernoulli effect, actually creating a vacuum behind the sphere to draw the exhaust out and indirectly forcing air into the intake. I saw that plane fly and, as it buzzed the field, one could see that it was really fast and maneuverable. I heard that the Navy got that one, but I never saw a subsequently developed plane which resembled it.

Standing in front of the headquarters at Yokota was a Kamikaze aircraft. It had droppable wheels (not landing gears), and was sleek and tiny. It was fascinating to think that someone would actually ride in this, with only enough gas to reach a destination, and then destroy himself by crashing the propellered bomb (armed just prior to takeoff) into a target. Some of these aircraft were used to bomb Okinawa. We actually saw one of these bomb that city from our vantage point on Ie Shima. It was scary.

C-46 Curtiss Commando

Upon first being assigned to Yokota, we began flying the C-46. There were no transitional training sessions. We were supposed to immediately know how to fly the aircraft, sometimes not necessarily affectionately called "The Whale." One characteristic of the C-46 was much appreciated as we were flying over water. If it went down over the sea, it could be rather easily landed,

A C-46 at Yokota.

A P-51 Mustang flying on my C-46's wing.

Flight Officer Vaughn at the controls of a C-46 at Yokota.

first because of its belly configuration. In addition, because of its integral fuel tanks in the wings and the bottom storage compartments, it would float. It had been reported that there were a number of C-46 derelicts which floated for so long that the Navy had to shoot them to destroy them!

Lieutenant Tait and Flight Officer Curtis beside a C-46 at Yokota.

The C-46 was not an easy plane to fly, even though it had servo-mechanisms to operate the controls. This was another case of a plane which should be piloted by a larger person (certainly not a small 5-foot, 6-inch such as I was). I wrote home about the C-46 on 17 October 1945:

A photograph of the Kimpo Airdrome in Seoul, Korea, taken while on cargo flight (note the curved building).

Well, here I am on my maiden voyage in a C-46. It is quite different from B-24s. Flies just about as hard. I am not particularly fond of it, but I imagine I will soon swear by it. When I first got into 24s I said I would never like them, but since I have left them, I've realized how good they were.

Flights were made, among other places, to Sapporo on the island of Hokkaido where we landed between snow banks taller than the C-46 itself. It was blindingly white all around, and it was difficult to determine perspectives. We stayed in barracks which were covered with snow and walked through tunnels of snow between buildings.

On one trip, we flew to Seoul, Korea, and, as I recall, one time to China. At the "Kimpo Airdrome" in Korea, there were a tremendous number of Japanese airplanes, mostly Zeros, lined up, awaiting some fate. They were in various stages of disrepair, some apparently having been cannibalized for parts prior to the end of the war. I understood that before surrender the Japanese were supposed to remove propellers from airplanes. That was not done in Korea. Because of our flight schedules we never did have an opportunity to explore Korea.

Flight to Biak, New Guinea

Our C-46 flying assignments were anything but "milk runs." We went to many areas throughout the Pacific, including Biak, New Guinea (northeast of Australia). We had to sleep on the plane there, for they had no available barracks.

I was so impressed by the tall coconut palm trees. They appeared to create a Gothic cathedral. However, we were warned that we should not venture far from base, for the New Guinea natives were not friendly and had a history of cannibalism. Whether this was true or not, fortunately I am not certain. I did see some of them and they had very large hairdos, larger than most of the Afros of more recent years. They were derogatorily called "fuzzy wuzzies." Apparently, there was little if any association between them and the Americans.

In all of our flights with the C-46, there were absolutely *no* navigators. We flew by dead reckoning (there's that strange term again) and by radio compass, even for the flight from Yokota to Biak, New Guinea (approximately 13,000 miles as the "crow flies"). In a 28 October 1945 letter to my family, I wrote about the trip to Biak:

I've just returned from a ten day tour of the Pacific (as Eleanor Roosevelt would put it). We were empty to Biak. It was my first flight

Japanese airplanes at Kimpo Airdrome.

Atsugi Air Base, Japan, from a C-46 in landing pattern.

as co-pilot in the 46. It is a difficult plane to fly in one sense, however, I don't mind it. We left Yokota, Japan (5 hours), then to Yontan, Okinawa (stop overnight), next was Clark Field, Philippine Islands (6 hours), stayed overnight there, flew to Pelelu [Palau] overnight (in the Peleu chain next to Angur Is. — 5½ hours), then to Biak, D.N. Guinea (3 hours). We picked up 21 passengers there. We landed at an "Aussie" airstrip and they invited "us old chaps, in fer a spot o' tea." We took off immediately and back to Pelelu (3 hours), known as the "Airtel of the Pacific." Stayed overnight. The next morning we had mag [magneto] trouble that held us up for four days. We flew from there to Guam (5½ hours) and to Iwo Jima (4½ hours) in the same day. Bad weather held us up there for another day. 4½ hours took us to

Atsugi [Japan] where we were rid of our cargo and passengers. Then 20 mins. and we were here [Yokota].

There were no navigators available to us, because they needed fewer points in order to return to the States for separation. As a result there was a shortage of navigators in the Pacific. They were not really needed when flying transports from island to island, as long as there was a competent pilot and co-pilot. The trip to Biak was made without navigators and involved several stops. Usually when we landed it was too late to take advantage of mess hall hours. As a result, we carried individual supplies to carry us over (usually C-Rations). During any trip to the South Pacific, we always looked forward to landing at Palau because it was under Navy control, and they had all the good things — fresh vegetables, steaks, eggs, and other food, liquor, nurses, dances, etc. On another trip back through Palau, as previously mentioned, we had to replace a magneto on one of the engines. They had no magnetos for the C-46 and had to fly one in from the Philippines. We felt happy that we were stranded there for a few days unscheduled R & R, and *not* in Biak or some such other place.

Military planes of all types, combat as well as cargo, were not designed with bathrooms. Instead they had, with male personnel in mind, relief tubes to accommodate *nonserious* relief. For more serious needs, flight crews used empty waterproof C-Ration boxes. This posed no real problem as long as the flight crew and passengers were male, and we were transporting supplies. When transporting female passengers such as nurses, however, there *was* a problem. And what a problem! They not only had to use the C-Ration boxes as we used the relief tubes, but they filled the boxes to overflowing with *serious* and *nonserious* deposits. What else could they do? With a full load of nurses, that in itself left little room for accommodating the rough turbulent air which we sometimes encountered. Imagine that mess and what had to be done when we reached our destination on another tropical or subtropical location.

It may seem irresponsible for us to have risked flying passengers (nurses) for long distances over water when we had no navigator aboard. Perhaps it was; but when flying over water, it was rather easy to spot an island, where there were almost always cloud formations which could be seen for hundreds of miles (depending upon the size of the land mass). In addition, practically all of the destination islands had range and broadcasting radio. Our radio compasses usually could home into them, unless there was radio interference from lightning. At any rate, we were not concerned about not having a navigator. It worried others more than us.

On the trip back from Biak, we landed at Iwo Jima. I wrote to my family on 28 October about visiting that island:

We met some Sea Bees on Iwo who moved in with the assault troops of Marines, and they showed us the island — drove us to the top of Mt. Surabachi where we saw the monument to the erection of Old Glory there. You know that mountain is an active volcano. Usually when you go to the top of a mountain, it gets cold, but on old Surabachi, it is very warm and you can see the steam and sulphur there. The fortifications on Iwo are terrific, concrete-reinforced pillboxes lined the beach and hills. The landing troops were under the cross fire of the Mountain and the hills. It was all very interesting. They had one big block house with a wall of about two yards thick. They were prepared all right!

Russian Threat

During our stint at Yokota, there was a threat that the Russians were planning to come to Japan and to occupy part of the territory that was now held by the United States. It should be noted that the USSR did not declare war on Japan until 8 August 1945 (about three weeks after the detonation of Trinity in White Sands, New Mexico, and two days after the bombing of Hiroshima). Because of the very real threat of possible USSR invasion of Japan after it had been occupied by the United States, we were put on full alert at Yokota. That threat would appear to have been real, for it should be kept in mind that when the first American occupation troops landed, there was a Russian Navy officer present alongside the Japanese officer.

Military discipline was fully enforced. Once during this alert I was stopped by the MP because I was not carrying my sidearm (.45 pistol). We posted guards around the perimeter of the base. One night when I was Officer of the Guard, I was making my rounds and found that one of the guards had simply walked off from his post and, as I recall, went into town. As a result, there was a Court Martial, and I was one of the testifying officers. He was found guilty and went to the stockade, but I don't recall for how long. The possibility of a Russian invasion was continuing scuttlebutt all around, especially from the Japanese. I remember one time when Papa Tsugumo said, "You will have trouble with the Russians. They are not to be trusted. We learned that years and years ago." He was so right. But the Russians did not invade Japan, fortunately, though we were preparing it.

Tachikawa

I was transferred from Yokota to Tachikawa in November 1945. I was also transferred from the 2nd Combat Cargo Group to the 317th Troop Carrier Group. At that time Tachikawa was a much larger base than Yokota. It had a long airstrip, for it was the factory where many of the Japanese aircraft were

Tachikawa Air Base, Japan, Main Gate.

assembled. The flight line was framed with bombed-out factories and hangars. The barracks were two-story wooden-framed buildings, neither attractive nor comfortable. At the same time, they were not really safe, for we had oil-burning space heaters. As might be expected, one cold night, there was a fire in our barracks and it burned to the ground. I lost a lot of things, including many photographs, but especially my precious air mattress (which I had acquired on Ie Shima, trading my cigarette and beer rations for it).

After being transferred from Yokota to Tachikawa, most of us were assigned ground duty, and flew only enough to get flight pay. I was assigned as the Managing Officer of the Officers Club. The Club building itself, when I assumed the management, was an ugly, decrepit old veterinarian school building, which had been cursorily transformed into an Officers Club. The financial condition of the Club was a disaster, as was evidenced by the monthly assessment made to each officer. I discovered that the financial records were in complete chaos, so I took them to the Air Inspector. We then started all new books, with the financial balance starting with what was there at the time. They were considering recalling the former officer, and have him give an accounting, for it appeared that considerable funds were unaccounted for (fortunately for him, they never followed through). After that, the cash reserves of the Club began to climb. They climbed so much that we had to have "free" nights at the Club, including all drinks and all food. Broiled steaks simmered in champagne was the specialty of Mr. Jimmy, our Chef "borrowed" from the Hotel New Grand in Yokohama. We started to have an

The Officers Club (called the "317 Club") in Tachikawa where Flight Officer Vaughn was the manager.

The staff of the Officers Club and Flight Officer Vaughn, Tachikawa.

orchestra in for dances and eventually we discontinued the assessment altogether.

During my travels around the area of Yokota and Tachikawa, I was told by a number of people that American fliers were beheaded in a nearby shrine. I do not, however, recall which shrine. One would have to examine the larger

Chef "Jimmy" (formerly at the Hotel New Grand in Yokohama) and Flight Officer Vaughn at the Officers Club in Tachikawa.

shrines to discover where the actual burial site was located. As I remember, it was on a road which made a 90° turn after the shrine, in a level rather than a hilly area. I was told that the people who were beheaded were officers, and they were accorded an honorable death and burial in accordance with Japanese military custom.

Chapter 5

Japan —
Occupation Discoveries

The most beautiful thing we can experience is the mysterious.
It is the source of all true art. . . .

Albert Einstein
What I Believe (1930)

Discovering Japan

Immediately upon arrival in Japan, I was determined to learn as much about this beautiful country as I could. Although the beauty of the countryside was obvious where war had not reared its ugly head, the beauty of the people and their culture was not as evident without further discoveries. Much of what I discuss here is from personal experience and assumptions on my part, and not necessarily from academic research. As such, one should not take my word as "gospel," for it is anything but that. Part of the basis for this section is from correspondence home to my family. Other parts are from my monograph, and others are from memory. If there are contradictions or errors in fact or assumption or omissions, they are not intentional.

The story which I am relating does not necessarily follow chronological sequence in discovery. It does not include material relating to the House of Tsugumo, as that is treated in Chapter 6. In addition, this portion of my narrative does not generally relate to military assignments, but is, instead, the occupation experiences chosen by me, or accidentally thrust upon me as a result of my choices.

Transportation and Distance

The Japanese railway system was a marvel, especially when one considers how much damage it must have suffered from the bombings and the resulting continual repairs. The trains were called *densha,* and were very reliable. Because we military personnel did not have to pay a fare, travel was facilitated. In addition, with some access to military vehicles, and by combining trips with others, we had a limited but adequate transportation system. Most of my exploring of Japan involved day trips out of Yokota or Tachikawa. As a result, the distances covered and places visited were limited to those environs.

The distances (and resulting area) are relatively small, and as such one should not draw the conclusion that the rest of Japan was similar. The following are very cursory approximations of some of the railway distances traveled: Ome to Yakota (Fussa City) — 5 miles; Yakota to Tachikawa — 7½ miles; Tachikawa to Ome — 12½ miles; Tachikawa to Hachioji — 4 miles; Tachikawa to downtown Tokyo — 25 miles; Tachikawa to Hino — 2 miles; Tachikawa to Hanno — 15 miles.

Fortunately, I followed a path, albeit sometimes unplanned, which lead to broadening my mind, to gaining friends whom I consider as family, and to learning about Japanese language, art, culture, religion, and history. This was in contrast to what military personnel should have done. We were instructed by the military authorities not to fraternize with the Japanese, that they could not be trusted, and that there might be grave danger in associating with them. We were instructed not to eat their food for fear of intestinal disorders, and also because there was a shortage of food immediately after the war. We were commanded to carry our .45 pistols at all times. We were not permitted to marry Japanese girls. The only way one could marry a Japanese girl was to obtain permission from the Commanding Officer. I recall when discussing it one time with someone in Headquarters, probably the Adjutant, he said, "The Commanding Officer has never granted permission for an American to marry a Japanese, and I know he never will." For that reason, most relationships between Japanese girls and American soldiers were either platonic, or in violation of the fraternization edict, or without serious commitment at that time. I would assume that this mandate changed after I left Japan — in my opinion, it certainly should have.

As a result of the military mandate, most officers did not venture off base at the beginning. However, on my second day, I left the base at Fussa and discovered the little town of Ome. It became a second home to me. At that time, I wore my .45 pistol sidearm. That, of course, did not bode well to make friends with the Japanese. It did, however, give me confidence (I was a marksman with the .45, and considered myself to be a good shot).

The matter of language was a barrier and a problem initially for Americans who would venture out, for we were not prepared to try to communicate with the Japanese. It should be remembered that Yokota is a small town in the country area and Ome is a smaller town located in an even more isolated mountain area. As such, it should have been obvious that it would be difficult to communicate with the Japanese.

The Role of Tea in Japan

Tea was an integral part of the Japanese life, apparently even much more so than it was for the English. Everywhere one went, tea was offered. In spite of the mandate not to partake of Japanese food, from the very first I felt confident in drinking the tea, for the water was always boiled before it was poured on the tea leaves. I did not always feel that confident about food, especially in some of the places where I went, except where I had been before, and where I knew they understood my concern. The importance of tea as an historical social custom is epitomized in the practice of the classical "tea ceremony." The tea ceremony was performed once for me by Mama Tsugumo (whom I also called Okasan), utilizing powdered tea and extremely old and interesting dishes and utensils.

Sometime later I learned that the tea ceremony originated with the Buddhists, apparently some time in the fifteenth century. This ceremony appears to take the nature of a sacrament in the Christian tradition, but in this case involves making and serving tea to the guests. Very formal and traditional Japanese politeness and courtesy are displayed through the preparation of the utensils, the chamber, the mixing of the tea, and its serving and consumtion by the participants.

After the ceremony, Mama Tsugumo asked me what I thought of it. In my youthful nonchalance, I said I did not understand it, and, of course, I did not. The military did not provide any guides to the history and culture of Japan, or at least to us. If they had, it is almost certain that the tea ceremony would have been explained, since it was such an important part of the culture and custom of the governing class. Perhaps, it was not a part of the occupation program by default because of the general confusion at that time.

Not everyone is an expert in performing the tea ceremony, and, as I understand, it was originally the province of the classical Geishas, as it took years of training to learn properly. I would presume that the modern version performed by other persons of lesser experience and training might not be as culturally accurate as it formerly was.

Fujiyama

It would be irreverent, even unthinkable, not to mention the presence of Fujiyama first whenever discussing discoveries in Japan. When flying into Yokota it is impossible to miss seeing this majestic mountain. There are three

Mount Fuji (Fujisan, Fujiyama) in "classical pose," taken from the window of a C-46.

photographs in this memoir which display some of the majesty of Fujiyama, although one of them might be considered as irreverent because of the closeness of the image of Fujiyama's crater. I took the photo "Fujiyama in a classic 'pose' " from a C-46. The other two photos were taken by a friend with an aerial camera.

I had an encounter with Fujisan which forced respect for this venerable

Mount Fuji "straight ahead."

mountain. One time I was a co-pilot on a flight to Korea, and because I was to fly after we left Japanese air space and with the flight engineer in my co-pilot's seat, I was taking a nap on the cloth seats which lined the perimeter of the cabin (it had been a late night for me as manager of the Officers Club). When we approached Fujiyama, it became rather turbulent. What I did not know was that the pilot planned on flying directly over the mountain. Had I known that I would never have been so complacent as to try to sleep. I can tell you that my rest was severely interrupted when we started to pass over Fujiyama. I was flung up against the cabin ceiling so hard that it bruised my head and broke my shoestrings. My shoes went flying across the cabin. I had respect for Fujiyama before, and after that flight, I had even more.

My First Japanese Discoveries — Fussa and Ome

Early on I ventured from the base alone, I guess, due to the ignorance of youth. Others did not want to go along. To get anywhere from the base, one had to pass through the small town of Fussa, home of Yokota. A description of the geisha house between Yokota and Fussa is found in my monograph:

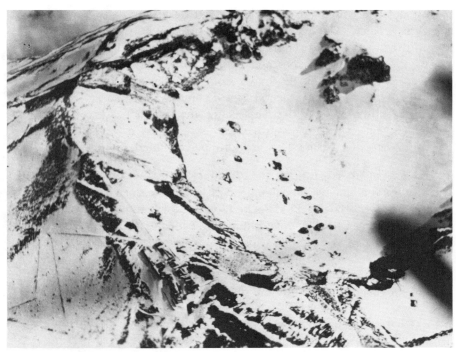

Mount Fuji bird's-eye view "from the top."

Our little airbase, Yokota, which is located near the town of Fussa, stood out like a skyscraper because of all the rice fields, and vegetable gardens surrounding it. There is one little group of buildings nearby, and one soon learns their "raison d'etre." This group of houses is what is known as the geisha house. It was built during the war, with the intention of keeping the Japanese soldiers happy. As we understand, it used to have its upkeep paid for by the Japanese Army. Now, as before, it was their aim to make the soldiers happy. Whenever one would walk down to the train station and pass there, the girls would invite any of the soldiers in. The place did a roaring business, and it was not bothered by the officials at the camp for about four months. The reason that they did finally place it off-limits, was the usual one. It wasn't closed because it was against the law (incidentally, General MacArthur put out an order stating that all geisha and houses of prostitution will be closed), but rather because too many of the soldiers were acquiring V.D. It has been reported that several places were kept open, by the M.P.'s because they were allowed to frequent these places free of charge. Such is the racket that existed in new old

Japan. There was no difference as far as attitudes of officers or enlisted men. There were houses for officers only, and houses for enlisted men only. It seems as if the Japanese knew that the services would object to officers and enlisted men frequenting the same places. It should not be drawn from this that all geisha girls are prostitutes. There are several types, some that just serve food and drink in high class restaurants, some that just act, some that just dance, etc. The geisha profession used to be a very respected profession, but during the war it dropped its standards.

I walked past this institution and came into the town itself. Somehow, I was able to communicate with the people in Fussa, and learned a couple of words. When I first ventured out, I did not know where I was going. At the suggestion of a Japanese person who spoke English, I headed for Ome (the name means plum blossom). My first trip to Ome led me to a girls school, where I met the principal, who arranged for a translator. I wrote my family the following on 8 October 1945 (note: where I used "us" I really meant "me" and was implying a unity between the translator and myself):

> On my second day here I went to Ome. . . . I saw girls marching from school — there's a picture in one of the *Time* magazines [similar to what I saw there]. All the girls are dressed in black and marching in perfect step with no one leading them. I went to the school gates and all the girls turned and snickered. I guess I was the first man outside of teachers who had gone there. I stopped a cute little girl and asked her if it was all right. She couldn't speak English but showed us to the door and called the principal. The girls all bow before they leave the gates of the school. I had to take my shoes off before entering the school. They offered me a pair of sandals, but I couldn't get them on for a strip went between the big toe and the rest of it didn't fit. He showed me into his office and we sat down in some easy chairs and a girl made tea there and brought us some. It was very delicious. He [the principal] showed us around school — very much like our own. The auditorium was divided into rooms and he said they had to do that because of the war. It reminded me of the excuses . . . [we] used at home. There were three others who could speak a little English. They were happy to have us and treated us very nicely.

I was fairly certain that because of the fine treatment which I had been afforded on my first trip out, I had to make many more visits, and especially back to Ome. Later, I did make many more visits to Ome, and I wrote an account in my monograph of visiting a shrine there:

Flight Officer Vaughn in front of the Mitake Shinto Shrine near Ome, Japan.

御嶽神社（武州御嶽）の鳥居

The Mitake Shrine near Ome (pre-World War II postcard).

The other day I went to Ome and climbed one of the mountains overlooking the town. They had steps leading up and I was worn out when I reached the summit. There was a huge granite monument and a shrine in the clearing. A home was located nearby. The lady came out and went back in. She saw I was tired, and I walked up to the door and she asked me to sit down (in Japanese). . . . Then she made me a hot drink [of] water and [dried] flowers, probably cherry blossoms or roses [more probably plum blossoms, since Ome means plum blossom]. I was expected to drink the drink and eat the flowers, and strangely enough it was delicious. She gave me a little fan as a present.

Through the years I have saved a number of prewar postcards illustrating scenes of Japan's wonders prior to the war. One of these cards appeared to be the scene where the preceding visit took place. It also was similar to some photographs which I have included in this narrative (included in this chapter and in Chapter 6). I was not certain for I had never had the printing thereon translated, neither in Japan where I acquired it nor in the U.S. In May 1990 Tsuyoshi Suzaki, an instructor of the Japanese language at the University of the Virgin Islands, confirmed that the shrine illustrated on the postcard is the Mitake Shinto shrine on Mount Mitake, near Ome. I believe it is the one I visited and described in the preceding paragraph.

One of my very fondest memories of Ome was when it was misty in the twilight with halos around whatever lights there were. I could hear the muted sounds of families living there and to experience the smells, often of fish being prepared. The most special sound, however, was the clack clack of *getas* (platform wooden shoes) sloshing through the standing water. Because one could not see at a distance in the mist, it was fascinating to hear the sound increasing as someone approached and came into view, and then diminish as the person disappeared into the mist.

Tokyo

One would think that a person such as myself, so close to Tokyo, would have spent most of his time visiting it. Such was not the case. Although I did visit, I did not spend much time there, especially not in the commercial district. Our trip to Tokyo involved using the electric train, the *densha*, and making several transfers. It was truly an all-day adventure to go there from Ome or Tachikawa. As I recall on my first trip, we went to Tachikawa by train, changed trains, and transferred at Shinjuku to the subway. I wrote to my parents on 8 October 1945:

Destruction near Tokyo on the way to Shinjuku Station taken "on the run" from window of the commuter train (*densha*).

Flight Officer Vaughn at the moat in front of the Imperial Palace in Tokyo.

Perhaps you are interested in Tokyo. We had a very interesting trip there. We changed to the express at Tachikawa and it took about an hour. We passed very much destruction. Everyone says "B-29" [it is interesting to me that they never said "B-24" although the B-24 did some bombing there] and points out the window. You cannot imagine the amount of wasted [bombed out] area there is. Tokyo is terribly destroyed. There are some sections, however, that are still very nice. The Imperial Palace is surrounded by an old moat and our guide (in

The *Ginza* across from the PX (*Guinjin Kaikan*), Tokyo, Japan.

Tokyo) said one of the bombs hit in the water and destroyed or killed most of the fish.

The stores there close for the noon hour so everyone can eat his rice and drink his tea. I talked to quite a few persons who could speak English fluently. You can always bump into someone who can speak English and who has been in the U.S.A.

My travels to Tokyo city itself were relatively few, for I found the countryside and its people much more intriguing. While in Tokyo, I visited several "touristy" locations. One of them was the *Ginza,* which did not impress me. We looked for a Japanese-English, English-Japanese dictionary there, but they did not have one. They said all were destroyed in the bombing and fires.

Everyone had to have his photograph taken in front of the Imperial Palace. I was no exception. Another place, which was more impressive for nationalistic reasons than sheer beauty or majesty, was the American Embassy. It appeared to be fully intact, but we were not allowed to visit it. As a matter of fact, we could not walk on that side of the street, and there were guards all over. It seemed good to see the Stars and Stripes flying over the building. It seems strange also that it was not damaged by bombs.

"Old Glory" again flying over the American Embassy, Tokyo.

I saw the Toho Theatre, and it was not too badly damaged. It was being repaired and the name was being changed to "The Ernie Pyle Theatre." Fritz Henle, in *Das Ist Japan,* has a photograph of the Toho Theatre taken in the 1930s, and it did not look that much different from my photograph taken in 1945 after the war.

Across from the Toho Theatre there was a place where visiting servicemen always went — the *Guinjin Kaikan* (soldiers' store) or PX. There was still the ban on eating Japanese food at that time, so this was a place where we could

Toho Theatre, Tokyo, renamed at that time "The Ernie Pyle," 1945.

obtain "approved" food and Coca Cola. It was also a place to get directions to other parts of the city from English-speaking personnel.

There are many shrines in Japan, and it was obvious that they were important in the life of the people. I wrote about a shrine in Tokyo in my monograph:

> There is a beautiful shrine in Tokyo, the Yasukini Shrine. It is more like an American park than a shrine. The shrine was "off-limits" to American servicemen, and there were M.P.s stationed at the gates to keep out the curious Americans. I did not get inside, but I did get up to a fence and took a photograph of the huge "toro" or stone lanterns in front.

It became apparent to me many years later why the Yasukini Shrine was off-limits. Apparently, it was the official state Shinto shrine dedicated to the war dead. This was outlined in 1973 in an article by Robert Trumbull, a reader, in the 16 August 1973 edition of *The New York Times.* Trumbull indicated that there was a commotion when the Emperor and Empress made their appearance at official memorial rites on the 28th anniversary of the end of World War II. Veterans' groups led street demonstrations requesting that the government

Staff Sergeant Ward and Flight Officer Vaughn in front of *Guinjin Kaikan*, January 1946.

reestablish official status for Yasukini, a Shinto shrine revered as a place of refuge for the souls of the war dead. Government support for the shrine was abolished under the American occupation. Trumbull stated that the shrine, "was established in 1869 as the eternal resting place of the souls of those who died in defense of the empire."

The Imperial Hotel, Tokyo.

Mitaka

While stationed at Tachikawa, a friend of mine, Lieutenant Turner (isn't it strange how one sometimes forgets first names, and often writes last names down in photo albums) and I traveled around a bit. He had met some friends, the Takios family, who lived in Mitaka. Mr. Takios was an aeronautical engineer and had been involved with the development of new and experimental aircraft in Tachikawa. Lieutenant Turner and I spent some enjoyable hours with them in their lovely home in Mitaka. It was another opportunity to learn about the Japanese people, their culture, and their language.

The gates of the Yasukini Shrine, Tokyo.

The Yasukini Shrine "through the fence."

Tachikawa

Tachikawa was the scene of many of my adventures. It was there that we obtained film, usually Fuji or Sakura film, and where we had our developing done. Perhaps it is because of the professional care and attention that the negatives developed there are still in such relatively good condition.

There were shortages of everything after the war, and the Japanese being inventive were able to "make do." They made drinking glasses out of old beer bottles. They made toys and other things out of tins from canned food and flower vases from beer bottles. In addition, they established an unofficial market, which we called a "black market." A new *torii*, or gate, was hastily erected at such an area and carried the inscription of "The New Promotion of Tachikawa Stallmen's Association."

Mrs. Takios, Lieutenant Turner, and Flight Officer Vaughn at the Takios home, Mitaka, Japan.

Mr. and Mrs. Takios, and Flight Officer Vaughn at the Takios home.

A Tachikawa street scene.

At one time, we set out to locate a dam that we saw from the air, which was
near Tachikawa. I did not identify the dam by name when writing about it, but
I would assume that it might have been Yamaguchi or Murayama dam. The
following is my account of that adventure from my monograph:

Two friends, Lt. Fisher and F/O Curtis, and I took a weapons
carrier one Sunday, and went for a ride. We had all seen a reservoir
nearby, from the air, so we decided to take a look at it from the ground.

"The New Promotion of Tachikawa Stallmen's Association" *torii*.

Lt. Fisher drove and we headed in the direction of the reservoir. We became lost. . . . We finally stopped to ask someone where the reservoir was, and we ran into language problems. We didn't know the Japanese name for reservoir, so [at my suggestion] we said "Toxon mizzu" which means "Much water." In response to this, a man came out of the house carrying a dipper of water. He thought we wanted water for the truck. We finally got the point across, and he directed us to it. . . .

As we approached the reservoir's dam, we were impressed with the stone work on the dam. It appeared that each stone must have been chosen with care for the particular spot. Near the dam there was a beautiful modern house, apparently unoccupied, and there was evidence that it was recently occupied by G.I.s [beer bottles, etc.]. We went out on the control tower and took some photographs. We crossed the dam over a road which is primarily for one car, but it is wide

A bridge over the reservoir near Tachikawa.

enough for three or four. In the center is a smooth concrete strip wide
enough for one car. On the edge of this strip is a strip of cobblestone. It
was evidently placed there to aid a person in crossing the dam in a
black out.

Fathers Chiesa, Paganini, and Boano, Italian priests of the Society of St. Paul, Nakano, Japan.

Religion

The contrast between an overwhelming predominantly Catholic country like the Philippines and an Oriental religion country such as Japan was a revelation to a rather naive person of my age. During my stay in Japan, I had the pleasure of meeting many people, and especially those who were not Japanese but were from other areas, who were in Japan during the war. Many

Father Chiesa and Flight Officer Vaughn in Nakano.

Father Chiesa and children in Nakano.

of these were missionaries, although I saw practically no churches. Obviously any person not Japanese would have had a difficult time during the war, but probably more of a problem during occupation, because they would have been "neither fish nor fowl." I refer especially to those who were civilians and diplomatic corps members whom I met, such as those from Italy, Germany, Russia, etc.

One group I met made an indelible impression on me — the group of Catholic missionaries from Italy. Their religious order was The Society of St. Paul, and they were involved in the spreading of the word of God through the media. Their society in Japan was primarily involved with the printed medium. In other areas, they were involved with the cinema, as well as radio (at that time there was no television). They were in Japan before and during the war. Although they and their religion existed alongside their counterparts in Oriental religions, they apparently did not have a very large following. Because of the nationalism surrounding Shintoism and even the nature of other old established Oriental religions such as Buddhism, it was natural that an xenophobic attitude would develop towards religions from other lands, especially when accompanied by strangers from other lands. It was in this setting that I became acquainted with this group of dedicated Catholic missionaries. I was rather religious during my pre-military youth and especially during the period covered in this narrative, and I was impressed with them.

I met a number of Catholic missionaries from three countries that I remember — France, Germany, and Italy. The following, from my monograph, relates to the missionary priests from Italy:

> On another trip to Tokyo with Lt. Stoney, I met a Catholic missionary. He was a priest who had been out to Yokota to say Mass on Sunday. He was now riding back to Tokyo with Stoney in the weapons carrier. He was Father Chiesa, an Italian missionary, and had been in Japan for about ten years. He lived in Nakano. It was a cold and dirty ride, so [upon arrival] he invited us in to wash up and have tea. I was impressed by the happiness of this man, and all the people there. He had a Japanese housekeeper and one of the seminarians was her son. There were, in this community, four priests, one lay-brother, and several seminarians. They all lived very simply and operated a printing plant. They were printing Catholic literature in Japanese. Formerly they had a large plant in Yotsuya, but it had been bombed during the war, and all that remained was a chimney. They had a hard life during the war and were having a hard life even now. They said that during the war, they were considered as enemies, and

how they were now being treated as defeated Japanese. Their superior had been put into prison during the war, for being suspected as a spy. They invited us to come back and visit them at any time.

A few days later, I went back there to visit them, and I had a very interesting visit. I went for a walk [with Father Chiesa] and the children all flocked around Father Chiesa. I took some photographs of these children. I was with them for Easter in 1946. I went to 10:00 Mass in which Fr. Paganini was the celebrant. I was impressed to see all the shoes lined up outside the church. Inside the church there were benches in the rear, and the usual straw mats in the front. On these mats were seated the congregation. The kimono-clad men seated on one side and the women on the other side. The women all wore silk scarfs over their heads. The church was in the hospital across the street from the seminary. A French priest was in charge of the church, and the Japanese sisters who sang the high Mass, were in charge of the hospital. The last time I went to visit the missionaries, Fr. Boano was directing the sisters in choir practice. During the practice, they had a small crippled baby in the crib, and they were taking care of it while practicing. It was impressive to hear these Japanese sisters singing the same words and music as we had at home, and the same as those all over the world. It was wonderful to walk into a church so far from home and feel "at home." The priests had a little Japanese truck, barely large enough for two people inside, and a motorcycle. They needed these things to get the type, paper, and all the things necessary for a printing plant. They said they could sell every book that they could print. All of their supplies had to be bought from the "black market."

Because these missionaries were in such dire need, I reluctantly gave them my Royal portable typewriter. I had previously bartered something for it at Yokota or Ie Shima. It was a welcomed addition to their meager holdings of printing equipment.

Due to the influence of this group of missionaries, I decided to go to their seminary on Staten Island after returning to the States. It was a time when I was able to readjust to nonmilitary life, to reaffirm my faith, and to get over whatever I had to get over after the war. It is interesting that a chance meeting in Japan had such a powerful influence on the rest of my life.

While there, I made application to Columbia University, was accepted, but was advised that it would be six months to a year before I could begin my studies. At that time I was 23 years old, and I felt I could not delay my education. I then decided to attend Ohio State University, in my home state, where I had preference over people from other states.

Mr. Omezawa (friend of Papa Tsugumo) at his home in Hachioji.

Hachioji

Hachioji was an area where I spent a considerable amount of time. When I was transferred to Tachikawa, Kunetoshi (Papa) Tsugumo, head of the Japanese family I came to love, gave me the name of a close friend of his who lived in Hachioji, which is near Tachikawa. This was an entré into another area of Japan, which I might not otherwise have seen, at least in the manner in which I saw it. I took the train from Tachikawa to Hachioji and asked a policeman to help me locate Mr. Omezawa whom I learned formerly had a silk mill there. The town was badly damaged from bombings, for there was hardly a building left standing. Mr. Omezawa's house, however, had not been hit by the bombs, but there were some craters in his yard. Mr. Omezawa was a very stout man, and he had an ivory cigarette holder which matched his build.

An interpreter magically appeared and I was able to communicate quite well with Mr. Omezawa, who invited me back for dinner. There were a large number of dishes, as is usual, and the meal was delicious. The main dish was chicken sukiaki. Mr. Omezawa asked me what year I was born, and I said 1924. He then produced a bottle of French cognac, vintage 1924. It was a

Hachioji Boys Middle School.

marvelous experience to meet another rather important Japanese person who spent time in helping me learn about Japan and its language, and I was fortunate that the interpreter was there and assisted me.

Afterwards, the interpreter accompanied me to the train station. He was an English teacher in a nearby school and asked if I would care to visit his home which was on the way to the train station. I readily accepted. His wife and son greeted me and offered me coffee. That was the first time I was offered coffee

Kamikaze "pilot-in-training" Michigi Bato and friend at home in Hachioji.

as I entered a home, rather than tea, and it must have been quite a sacrifice for them. I was invited to return to visit the interpreter's school, which I did later.

This school was the Hachioji Boys Middle School. The interpreter was conducting a class in advanced English which had several students. He greeted them in English, and they replied in English. I think they were pleased to be able to practice the language with me. One of them, who agreed to take me to the train station, also asked me to come back to Hachioji to visit his home. The next time I was going to Hachioji I met him on the same train, and he again asked me to visit his home on this visit. I did, of course, and the traditional tea was served. Later his father brought out the whiskey, which also was beginning to seem to be somewhat traditional.

In Hachioji I met a Kamikaze pilot-in-training, Michigi Bato. I met several of his friends, who apparently also were Kamikaze trainees. They were very ordinary type people with a real zest for life and a sense of humor (maybe that was a requirement). As a gift, Michigi presented me with some old, unusual Japanese coins.

At the railway crossing near the Hachioji Boys Middle School, we saw a very young boy, at a railway crossing guardhouse, who operated the gate. It seemed strange to see someone so young doing such a serious job. Another sight in Hachioji was the outdoor market, something like a flea-market, but with plenty of people, somewhat like the "Tachikawa Stallman's Association." I understand it was sort of a black market, which had sprung up to fill the needs created after the bombing. Hachioji was really a poor area after the war. It was busier than usual, however, because there was a festival in progress. One such festival, I recall, was the celebration of Hina Matsuri, or the Children's Festival (perhaps it could be called the Doll Festival).

In Hachioji I also visited a large shrine and cemetery, which I discussed in my monograph. I believe that it was the Gokurakuji Temple; the Master was Y. Ozawa and the boy was H. Fujita.

The railway-crossing guard at Hachioji.

A festival street scene in Hachioji.

One day while wandering around Hachioji, I came to a large shrine and a cemetery. I decided to look around. I wandered up to the center building, and saw a lot of young girls seated on the floor. I went around to the back of the shrine, and there I was greeted by a young man. He invited me to sit down and have a cup of tea. He could speak

Another view of the Hachioji festival street scene.

a little English, and with what Japanese I knew, we got along OK. I
asked about the shrine and he said it was a Buddhistic shrine. He
started talking and said he had been in the Army in China, and here he
was the house boy for the Buddhistic priest. He began to explain the

"Baby sitter" at the festival in Hachioji.

shrine. I asked him if I could look around, and he said he would be
happy to show me around. I was asked to remove my shoes. Then he
led me through a covered corridor to the temple proper. The young
girls were still there when we arrived. He explained that they were
holding classes there for their school had been bombed out. On the
black board they had several chemical equations. There was a central
altar, but it was almost barren. Beside the altar, there was a small stand
with a [huge] porcelain gong resting on a pillow. He picked up a
mallet and hit the gong several times. Then he handed it to me, and
asked me to hit it. It made an impressive sound. It seemed strange to
see a gong made out of anything but metal, and besides it was really
huge, making one wonder how it was ever manufactured. He led me
behind the altar into another room. There I saw many little gold
lacquered wooden tombstones. In front of all these markers were

Children "dressed up" for the Hina Matsuri festival in Hachioji.

many cups with what appeared to be tea in various stage of evapora-
tion. They [apparently] have a custom of keeping tea always available
for their immediate deceased relatives.

Hanno

Another adventure took me to a seemingly "distant" place. It was not the
intended destination of Nikko, but nevertheless proved interesting. Again,
time away from the base prevented me from continuing on. In addition, it
should be remembered that the Americans were still not permitted to partake
of Japanese food, and certainly there were no country inns where we could get
food and/or stay overnight in case we had time to go farther. Hanno was one of
these way-stops which resulted from this limitation. The following is from the
monograph:

"Boys at play" in Hachioji.

One day I decided to take the steam train to Higashifussa. It was about the only steam train that I saw in Japan. It took about four hours to go to Nikko. There was a huge Buddha there, and I planned on going there. After a few stops some more soldiers got on, and they said that military men need special passes to go from our area to Nikko. I decided to stop short of Nikko, and it so happens that I stopped in Hano [sic]. I looked around the area and I saw what looked like a factory across the railroad tracks. I ventured that way and passed a hospital. It was a dilapidated place and I can imagine that it was filled, for there were a lot of people around, we (another American [officer] joined me in "exploring" the scene) came to what was the remains of a factory which had manufactured lenses, cameras, and films. There wasn't much left of the place, and there were only a few guards around the place.

In the distance we saw a group of large buildings. These turned out to be a boys school. It was large and really a beautiful sight. As we approached, we were greeted by an interpreter who took us to the superintendent. The superintendent showed us around the school. It was very similar to American schools. This school was specializing in agricultural education, and everywhere one could see exhibits of farm products, animals, etc. Everywhere we went the students and teachers stopped class to look at us. As we left the students were hanging out of the windows, waving to us.

A Swiss-style chalet restaurant at Hino.

A lady gardener at the Swiss chalet, Hino.

I should point out that by this time, I had become "more proficient" in the spoken Japanese language. The written language, however, was an entirely different matter. There were a number of officers who would ask me to accompany them when they were going shopping, for I could negotiate a little

The Hanno Boys School of Agriculture taken from the train tracks.

bit for them. The language is not really difficult to pronounce, and it follows other phonetic patterns.

Hino

After the Army rescinded its restriction on Americans eating at restaurants Mr. Omezawa took me to a Japanese restaurant in Hino. It was obviously a high-class (*ichi bon*) restaurant in the setting of a Swiss chalet, somewhat similar to what might have been seen in the States at the time. There were quite a few well-dressed Japanese people and a few American officers (none of whom I knew). While the ambiance was of a Swiss chalet, the cuisine was not, although it was very good. I was adventuresome with food in Japan and as a result did not hesitate to try new dishes. I never will forget the fare that day, for it was whale meat served on bread made from fish eggs — very unusual.

Other Matters

Somewhere in my travels of discovery, I met people who said that during the war, the Japanese government officials were extremely anti-communist. The government would go into the house of an individual who was suspected of

The Hanno Boys School "close up."

being communist, an agitator, or a spy (I guess the modern communist term would be "hooligan") and would remove all the books with red covers. Because I heard this from several sources, I am inclined to believe it.

Also somewhere along the line I met some people who had a parrot. It seemed so strange to hear a parrot screeching out in Japanese *"Konnichiwa"* (hello). I had only heard parrots speak in English and this seemed amusing.

Any culture has its own humor and often only a knowledge of the language can allow the visitor to share it. The nuances of language, with word combinations, and even intonation all have an influence on the appreciation of humor. There were many times when the Japanese people would tell a joke, which I would not understand, in spite of the fact that they would obligingly translate it for me. Often, the translation would leave me wondering what was humorous about it. Such was the case about one joke which I heard several times from different people. Everyone would roar in laughter when they heard it. The joke was translated for me: "Why is salt fish salty? Because it swims in the sea."

Concerning financial matters, we were not permitted to invest in Japanese companies, stocks, or deposit money in Japanese banks. At the beginning, we also had to use occupation currency issued by the United States, which replaced the existing currency. This led to plenty of confusion and distrust of paper money. The Japanese were given a certain amount of time to convert their money into the new currency. As a result, there were many Japanese banknotes floating around which were worthless. It was not unusual to see people with handfuls of these worthless outdated notes trying to negotiate for their use. As a matter of fact, I still have a "short snorter" (a collection of paper currency notes attached to each other in a roll, upon which acquaintances would sign their names) with quite a number of large-denomination Japanese notes. While in Ie Shima, on 1 September 1945 I wrote my parents:

> The money situation here is rough. We have not been paid for two months, but we should be getting it soon. The value of money over here is going down. A yen when we arrived was worth ten cents, and now it's down to six cents. Before the war, it used to be worth 23 cents.

Parting Shot

For our reception in Japan I am grateful. Actually, the relationship between the Japanese and the Americans was a quandary at first. Wherever we went in Japan, the people who had been propagandized as to our brutality, etc. (as we were propagandized about them), were apprehensive whenever an American soldier — and especially a military officer, unexpectedly appeared. It must have been extremely difficult for them to have been so gracious to us when we had just fought a violent and bloody war. For their kindness and generosity, I am forever grateful.

Chapter 6

Japan — The House of Tsugumo

Peace be to this house.

Luke 10:5

Papa Kunetoshi Tsugumo

Kunetoshi Tsugumo is one of the "most unforgettable characters I have ever met." The unforgettable part of his character was his charisma, his ability to forgive and forget, his ability to make things happen, and his ability to coalesce his family into a unit, even while he was away. I knew Papa Tsugumo in a very personal way, as I have stated. I called him and his family "my Japanese family," for they veritably became that. Having been deprived of a close family relationship since the age of 17 because of the war, the adoption of a family relationship with people who cared, took me through a period of my life which might otherwise have been much rougher. It, in turn, affected my entire future life, in terms of philosophy, concern for others, looking for the different view, appreciating people around me, seeking art in nature, and understanding art in art.

This experience taught me to appreciate people from all areas, their cultures, and especially their languages. My decision to major in geography and in business administration, with an emphasis in foreign trade and international economics, stems largely from this experience. In addition, it resulted in the selection of a number of art courses as electives. The small experience of learning a little of the Japanese language encouraged me to study languages, especially French and Spanish, and partially encouraged me to write my doctoral dissertation on a largely unwritten French-based Creole language, from the island of St. Lucia in the Caribbean.

Papa Tsugumo in his library at home, Ome.

Originally in Japan, I called Papa Tsugumo "Sensei." Later because of the relationship that developed, I addressed him as "Papa." The title "Sensei" in some sense relates to the English title "Professor," or in a simpler purer sense "Teacher." While it is an honorable term, and one which demands respect, it

Above: Papa Tsugumo, 1963. Right: Papa Tsugumo's signature in Japanese (from his book of memoirs). (Courtesy of Taro Kikutani)

is still not encompassing enough as a title for Kunetoshi Tsugumo. In quoting passages from my letters and monograph, I have taken the liberty of uniformly using the term "Papa" in place of "Sensei" or "Mr."

Background

It is difficult to write a small biographic sketch of Kunetoshi Tsugumo, for he was a "big man" in many ways except physical stature. He was forceful, assertive, and deep voiced.

He was born in Ome in 1894. When I met him, he was about 51 years of age. He was a very active man, whose face always seemed to be smiling, but with a wistful expression of cautious optimism. Papa Tsugumo was elected to the lower house of the Diet (Congress) in 1928, at the age of 34. His political career extended through 32 years. He was an aristocrat, who was a member of the House of Peers (Senate). As a former Japanese military officer (I believe he was a General), he served throughout Korea and China, and perhaps other

Papa Tsugumo at Miyanohira. (Courtesy of Taro Kikutani)

Papa Tsugumo, Sensei Kikutani, and friend at Miyanohira. (Courtesy of Taro Kikutani)

places. These he described so very slightly to me. During his service in those areas, he certainly studied the heritage and birthplace of Japanese art.

Papa Tsugumo was a friend of the aristocracy of Japan. He was knowledgeable about all Oriental art, and, as a result, could be considered as a curator of at least a part of the National Treasures of the Imperial Household. He had, to my knowledge, three residences: one in Ichigaya near Tokyo, badly damaged by bombs which left only the storage vault of a former magnificent structure; the main family residence in Ome, which had a library, a reliquary for artifacts, and a third-floor theater/music room; and a rustic mountain retreat in Miyanohira, near a babbling, swift-flowing mountain stream.

Papa Tsugumo's wife, whom I called Okasan (Mama) Tsugumo, was a very talented, artistic, compassionate, and loving lady who revered her family and took great pains to guide them and care for them. Her dedication to making every meal a work of art, regardless of substance, was something to behold. She was someone who could always be relied upon. In the absence of her husband in her home, she took his place with dignity, charm, and friendliness. She was always cheerful. I loved that great lady, like my own mother. After

Flight Officer Vaughn and Mama (Okasan) Tsugumo at Ome.

Robert [Vaughn] signature in Japanese.

returning to the States and when I was in college, I learned that she had cancer. I was saddened to learn later that she had succumbed to the disease. She is gone, but she is not forgotten, nor will she be during my lifetime, and the lifetime of all of her children and her children's children — and I expect much beyond that.

Papa Tsugumo had several children, who were not often involved in my visits: one son (whose name I cannot recall), and three beautiful daughters, Namikosan, Totsurosan, and Fujikosan. All except Namikosan were attending school, apparently in Tokyo. Beautiful Namikosan was married to a handsome young man, Taro Kikutani, who was considered a part of the family.

Tarosan and Namikosan in Machida City, 1969. (Courtesy of Taro Kikutani)

They had a person in the household who performed the service of a man's man, a caretaker, a friend, someone who could be relied upon utterly, and I might add, a tall, very muscular man, Mr. Taira.

I do not know the whereabouts of any of the children except for Namikosan. She lives with her husband in their own home in Machida-City, Tokyo, where one of their sons and his family also live. One of their sons lives in the old family home in Ome, and Tairasan lives in the mountain retreat at Miynohira. I understand that the home site there has been completely renovated and has a formal Japanese garden constructed under the counsel of Papa Tsugumo.

Initial Encounter

I wrote in my monograph about my initial exploration related to the Tsugumos:

My two trips to Ome had given me much enjoyment [and confi-

Papa and Mama Tsugumo with Taro Kikutani, brother Taro Kikutani, and sister Namiko Kikutani and their family at the Kikutani residence in Machida. (Courtesy of Taro Kikutani)

Flight Officer Vaughn in Papa Tsugumo's garden at Ome.

dence] and I learned much about the Japanese. . . . The next trip to Ome proved to be my most interesting and my most valuable experience.

As I wandered through Ome's narrow winding streets, I saw a large building behind a beautiful stone wall. The building looked like a Japanese shrine, to me. I thought it would not be disrespectful if I went in and looked it over. Can you imagine the nerve and ignorance of a young 21-year-old officer alone in newly surrendered Japan casually ambling around the streets and buildings of a remote area, with only a .45-caliber pistol, no significant knowledge of the language, no substantial Japanese friends at the time, and no means of immediately contacting his base? Fortunately, I encountered responsible people who forgave me my nerve and ignorance.

I went through a little gate, and found myself in a very beautifully

Tirosan, Papa Tsu-
gumo's estate manager.

designed garden. The scene was hidden from view, and I was amazed
to find it there. As I was gazing at the scene, I had a feeling that I was
being watched. So I turned around and discovered two men there
[who] were staring at me. One was a huge muscular bald-headed man
and the other, a small man of distinction. I judged the first one to be

View of Papa Tsugumo's home from the garden, Ome.

the caretaker and the other one a priest of the temple. I suppose I should have felt some fear in that situation, but I was perfectly at ease. Keep in mind, that at that time it was the month of October, and that the war had just ended in mid-August.

I felt as if this were a place sheltered from the outside world. I turned to the two men, and the older one said in broken English, "What do you want?" I stated that I thought this was a temple or a shrine, and the older gentleman said it was not a temple, but rather his home. He invited me to tea. This occasion and the ones previous led me to wonder what sort of people we conquered. Everywhere in Japan I had been treated with the utmost courtesy. The older gentleman gave

Another view of Papa Tsugumo's home from the garden, Ome.

me his card, and I found his name was Kunitoshi [*sic*] Tsugumo. Then I started the conversation rolling, as best I could. It seemed the old gentleman had studied English many years ago, but could not recall it as he wished. His wife brought out the tea, and then he asked me to

Papa Tsugumo with his *Butsuzo-no-ma* in Ome. (Courtesy of Taro Kikutani)

Visitors to Papa Tsugumo's home in Ome viewing ancient statues of Buddha. (Courtesy of Taro Kikutani)

come back next Sunday for a real Japanese dinner, and to bring a friend if I wanted. I thanked him, again in my halting Japanese, and advised him I would be very happy to visit him on Sunday. I returned to camp feeling fortunate in having met someone really friendly in Japan.

The second visit to Papa Tsugumo's home in Ome was a memorable one which confirmed that there was much to learn about Japan and that I must attempt to learn it quickly, because inevitably I would be forced to leave the country. I related in my monograph:

My next visit to Ome, the following Sunday afforded me an opportunity to observe the best in Japanese manners. I was greeted at the door by the . . . gentleman himself, and an English interpreter. I was escorted into the library. I was surprised to find easy chairs and all the comforts of an American home. The leather upholstered chairs, were very comfortable, and gave one a feeling of being at home again. As soon as I had come in, I was served the traditional Japanese green tea. The tea was followed by little cups of Japanese saki. The cups contained about two thimble-fulls, and were filled from a steaming little vase-like pitcher. The saki was very tasty, and its own warmth was accentuated by being served hot. After being served saki, we were escorted into a small square room, that is commonly found in Japanese homes. On the mat covered floor there was a square table of beautiful red lacquer. This table was about a foot high, and naturally that meant that we were to sit on the floor to eat. Cushions were provided for everyone.

The dinner consisted of a large variety of dishes, each portion very small. It seems that variety is essential there. There were several salads, a fish dish, soup, and then the favorite dish of all Japanese was served. It was chicken skiaki [sukiyaki]. It is prepared before your eyes, from raw chicken, onions, vegetables, water, soya sauce, etc. The fish that I had was tempera [tempura] style, that is coated with flour paste and deep fried. At the end of the meal came the inevitable twins, cold boiled rice and green tea. A pressed seaweed was served with the rice, and one was to wrap this seaweed, called "*nordi*" around some rice with ones chopsticks. It was a task, but I got along admirably, considering that this was my first experience with chopsticks (called *hashi*). It was a wonderful meal, and was really filling. They begged my forgiveness for the poor meal, since they were unable to get the type of food they formerly had.

After the meal, we retired to the sitting room, and the . . . gentleman started to tell me about his collection of old statues, pottery, and pictures. His sitting room was lined with curios. One had but to walk into the room and he felt that he was in a museum. The older man had traveled all over the Orient. He had statues which he had collected in China, Burma, India, Manchuria, Java, etc. It was interesting to wonder how one man could know so much about any

The *Bisha Mon*, God of War (God of Battle), statue presented to Flight Officer Vaughn by Papa Tsugumo.

art, particularly Oriental art. Evidently he was some sort of a teacher, for everyone called him Sensei, which means professor or teacher. One of the teacher's remarks was "I'm sorry that so many American soldiers are buying imitations and are taking them back to their country, thinking that they have the genuine article." He then added, "I'm going to give you something that is not an imitation, and I will feel better, knowing that there is at least one American who is going back with something genuine. I am going to give you a statue of Bisha Mon. He is the God of Battle, and I think it is appropriate that I give it to you, one of the victorious American soldiers." That evening I went home carrying one of the most treasured articles that I have ever received.

Papa Tsugumo's inscription on the front and verso of the cover of the box housing Bisha Mon was made there in his home in front of me. That inscription, perhaps, may reveal why I was so readily accepted into the Tsugumo family. It was partially translated as: "When Robert, in the occupation Army, visited my house and garden, I learned he had visited shrines and temples nearby. I was so touched by the fact that he was so very interested in our culture. I, therefore, present this statue to him as our memorial." It was dated 11 November [1945], and signed by Papa Tsugumo. I do not know if he purposely selected that date, Armistice Day (now Veteran's Day), as the date upon which to make that presentation to me, but it is highly probable. The small wooden statue was from the Ashikaga Era, between 1372 and 1440.

In an 11 November 1945 letter to my parents, I later discussed another meal with the Tsugumos, which was a little different:

> When we sat down, he (his wife) served us Italian wine of very old vintage . . . (all their drinks are served in small cups — glasses — of about two tablespoons). Then we went upstairs to the drawing room, sat on pillows on the floor around a short table. Then we were served a small cup (as mentioned before) of Japanese whisky [sic]. Then we retired to the dining room sitting on the floor at a short table (all of this was considered the dinner). Then we were served hot saki — from his special stock. It is very much like the dandelion wine you make. Then came the food — turnips, potatoes, some sort of soya bean cake, all boiled together (a large bowl in the center, and you were served the first helping and helped yourself after that). I had my check out with the chop sticks — this was called *hashi*. Next little cups of brandy. Then came tempura, bean cake and corn boiled in oil which tastes similar to our mush. Then they served us cold boiled rice . . . and radishes and pickles — imported from Persia. The last dish was in a large glass goblet with cherries, beans and white transparent cubes (I don't know what they were made of). It was sweet and was the dessert. Then the Senator brought out a strange looking bottle, which his interpreter said was a bottle of Japanese whisky [sic] presented to him personally by the Emperor. This concluded the meal, except for afternoon tea and a real apple.

The Tsugumo family home in Ome became my home away from home. It was nearby, I felt at home, and in retrospect, perhaps I took advantage of their hospitality. I did, however, feel that they did not mind my becoming so attached to them. I can now imagine that originally it might have been an embarrassment for them to have to socialize with Americans so soon after such a bitter war. I think the embarrassment might have been implied when I was attending a cocktail party where the guests were diplomats — Japanese, Italian, German, French, and Russian. I did not speak any of those languages at that time and only had a smattering of Japanese to get by with. No one, absolutely no one, professed to understanding English, and I had to converse with them in Japanese (if I wanted to be a part of the group). After I spoke in Japanese, everyone was cordial and "civil." At one time, I had the honor of

The inscription by Papa Tsugumo on the outside cover of the box housing *Bisha Mon.*

being introduced to Prince Tokugawa (I am not certain of his first name). I believe that the Prince had been educated in the United States, having attended one of the Ivy League colleges and obviously understood English. However,

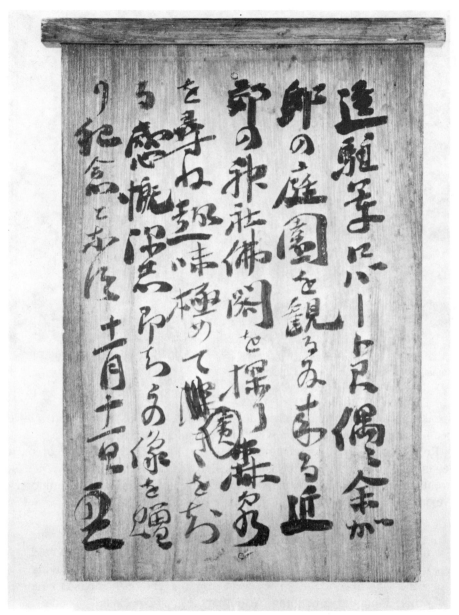

The inscription by Papa Tsugumo on the inside cover of the box housing *Bisha Mon*.

when I spoke to him in English, he ignored me; when I reverted to Japanese, he responded. Of course, I had no knowledge of Imperial protocol, and have since surmised that it must have been improper for a member of Royalty to

Mama Tsugumo and Taro Kikutani at Ome.

speak anything but Japanese on such occasions. Perhaps, it might also have been a political consideration when one considers the company.

Religious practices or customs are a part of the ordinary life of most Japanese. On one visit to the Tsugumos, I was privileged to experience an event which was amazing to me, one which I doubt many of my contemporary Americans experienced. I described it in my monograph:

> While visiting . . . [Papa Tsugumo's] home, I was amazed one night to see his son and his son-in-law open all the doors on a cold night, and run around the room, throwing beans around and saying something like "*skoh.*" They went from one end of the house to the other, doing the same thing. After that they came back and closed the doors. They explained that this was to chase the evil spirits out. After this ceremony was over, they took the remaining beans to the mother of the household. She gave each member one bean for each year of his life, and he was supposed to eat them. She had trouble getting the correct count for me, for I was twenty one, and according to the

Papa Tsugumo's mountain retreat with *To* and gazebo at Miyanohira.

Japanese method, I was twenty two. She was really confused, and gave me twenty three, instead. I told her about it, and she made me return one, for she said it would be bad if I got more than I was supposed to get.

Other religious or cultural evidence was learned through a visit to Papa

Sensei G. Nakajima (sometimes spelled Nakashima), noted Koto artist and father of Yasuko, with Flighter Officer Vaughn at the Nakajima home in Ichigaya.

Tsugumo's mountain retreat at Miyanohira. It was there that I saw a *To*, which was a pagoda-like stone monument. As I understand, a *To* has either 4, 7, or 13 eaves. Papa Tsugumo had erected a large one for his parents. It is a nice custom that the deceased are not immediately forgotten.

Sensei G. Nakajima, Mrs. Nakajima, and Yasuko at their home in Ichigaya.

Music

Music and art were an integral part of the lives of the Tsugumo family, and it was through them that I met many talented and famous Japanese musicians and saw theatrical presentations which otherwise I would not have had the opportunity to participate in, especially during the early "non-fraternizing" occupation period immediately following the end of the war.

At first I did not understand the music of Japan for it was so strange to me. I am not a musician, but as I understand it, much of the differences in the Japanese music results from what might be called a free scale instead of the 12-note scale of the West.

A sensational musical program at Yokota Air Base presented Japanese music in a manner which was accepted and partially understood by the Americans. Because all of the musicians were experts, there was no question about the quality of the performance. I wrote the following about that event in my monograph:

> One Sunday afternoon, Yokota Air Base was entertained by a program of classical Japanese music. . . . The entertainers were all

Yasuko Nakajima, daughter of Sensei G. Nakajima.

Yasuko Nakajima and Flight Officer Vaughn at Ichigaya.

professionals from Tokyo. In the program Professor Nakajima and his daughter Yasuko were the featured artists. . . .

Papa Tsugumo, also a member of the Japanese House of Peers, introduced the program, aided by his interpreter, Mr. Hobo. The program was unusual for the Americans to hear. There were different instruments such as the "sakuhachi," a flute-like instrument the "shamisen," a two-stringed banjo-like instrument, the "koto" [an instrument of between seven and thirteen strings, similar to a harp, but played in a horizontal position], mentioned previously [in a former letter], the violin, the piano. Miss Watanabe, a classmate of

Yasuko Nakajima and Flight Officer Vaughn playing a Koto duet (this photo appeared in a Japanese magazine).

Miss Nakajima, played the violin very beautifully. The program was well accepted by the audience. It was surprising to see so many Americans accepting the unusual classical Japanese music. There were many Japanese in the audience, for they were invited to attend also. In the audience was the little daughter of Papa Tsugumo, Fujico [Fujicosan]. Upon recognizing me, she rushed up to me and kissed me there in front of the whole audience. Fujico was about eight years old, and she was always happy to see me when I came to her home to visit her father. This simple display of affection by a child did much to show to the Americans that the Japanese were . . . very humane.

After the program, everyone was invited to inspect the Japanese musical instruments. It was surprising to see how many people went up to look at them. There was one American [Lt. Stoney] in particular who appeared very interested in the instruments. I had met him before. . . .

After examining the instruments and meeting the musicians, a group of us Americans were invited to join the musicians at the Tsugumo's home [in Ome] for a celebration. The musicians went on ahead, and we followed later by Jeep. Upon arrival we were ushered into the lovely sitting room where a hibashi was glowing. It was cold and the little fire felt good. We were first given tea, and then the traditional red rice, which is served only on special occasions. At first Lt. Stoney appeared afraid to eat it, but upon my example everyone tried it. It really was not too tasty, but because of good manners we ate it. After this, little Fujico came in and greeted all of us. She was the life of the party, and was very cute in her festive kimono.

We were then told that the music room upstairs was ready for us, and that we would have some music. Papa Tsugumo really had prepared for us, for he had some good whisky [sic] ready for us (and it was difficult, if not impossible to obtain). At least this was one way to keep warm. All of the musicians who had played at the base, played for us again, privately. After they had presented a program, they asked us to perform. I am no musician, but I thought it was necessary after all their efforts to please us. I gave a rather poor rendition of "Danny Boy," but apparently they appreciated my effort.

After being wined, dined, and serenaded, it was time for the musicians to leave, for they had to catch a train from Ome to be in Tachikawa by midnight, to catch the last train to Tokyo. It was almost too late for them to make it, so we bundled them all in the Jeep and took off for Tachikawa.

In my musical travels, through the influence of Papa Tsugumo and later that of the Nakajimas, I became more involved with Japanese music. In one visit to the Nakajimas, we arranged a fascinating visit to one of Japan's most famous musicians and composer, Miyagi Michio. That experience, as noted in my monograph, was unforgettable:

One day I was heading for Tokyo to see the Nakajimas, and I called over to Fussa to see if Lt. Stoney would care to go along. He decided to go, for I had a weapons carrier and we would not have to take the train. We were greeted royally by the Nakajimas. After some formalities we asked them to play something on the Koto. They granted our request, And we heard many famous old musical stories. Miss Yasuko was the only interpreter we had, and I must say that she did very well.

Papa Tsugumo, Totsuro Tsugumo, and Yasuko Nakajima at Ichigaya going to see Sensei Miyagi Michio.

It appears that she can use her English when she has to. Her father played something for us, and then Lt. Stoney tried to play the koto. He did rather well. It was impressive to see an American trying to play the koto. The Japanese people study the instrument all their lives, and here was Lt. Stoney, without any lessons, learning rapidly. I know that the Nakajimas noted his ability and they were taking a decided interest in teaching him. After several visits there, Stoney became an accomplished player [relatively speaking], and one of the Japanese newspapers came and took his picture. I later saw it in one of Japan's greatest newspaper. Lt. Stoney and I became acquainted with many musicians through the Nakajimas and Papa Tsugumo. We learned of the greatest koto artist [artist and composer] of all, Mr. Miyagi Michio, who was Yasuko Nakajima's teacher. We wanted to meet him, so we made arrangements with the Nakajimas to visit him. He lived on the South side of Yokohama, near Yokasuka and it would mean a long trip.

About a week later, we all packed in the weapons carrier on a very cold morning, and headed south. It was a long trip, and was very uncomfortable in the springless carrier. I drove down and for more reasons than one I was happy to get there.

Mr. [Sensei] Michio lived in an unpretentious house by the seaside on a hill. It was impressive in its quietness and the beauty of the landscape. One could hear the sea beating on the rocks below. I was rather surprised when I saw Mr. Michio, because he is a blind man. He certainly has done well, in spite of his handicap. I asked how he writes his music, and Yasuko said he plays the music and some member of the family writes it down. We were ushered into the sitting room, and we were all happy to place our feet under the *kotatsu* (a pit in the floor with a pot of charcoal burning under a grating). Over the pit in the floor is a small table, with a blanket covering it, and keeping the heat around our feet. Shortly after arriving, they started preparing our dinner. It was getting dark already, and we had to take so many side roads, we were in a hurry to finish. We had a very delicious meal of beef sukiyaki. After dinner we were served green tea. Then we asked Mr. Michio if he would play for us. A member of the family got out his koto, tuned it, and he tested it. He apologized for not having a better one, for his best one was in Tokyo. Two girls, apparently his nieces, played with him. One played a base koto, the other a cello-like koto, and Mr. Michio played the violin equivalent of the koto. They played several numbers, including "Seioto" which I had heard previously. Mr. Michio was the composer, and it was impressive to hear the number played as the composer intended. He also played "Sakura" variations (which he arranged) and Kazoyata variations. After Mr. Michio finished playing, he brought out his autograph album and asked us to sign it for him. It was an honor for us, for here are some of the names of people who had visited him and who had signed the same book: Mischa Elman, Helen Keller, G. Piatigorsky, Valentin Pavlovsky, Walter Schroder, Alice McFarland, Jennie M. Thomas, etc. It was getting late, and after thanking our host, we started back.

Musical Drama

The Nakajimas, and especially Sensei G. Nakajima whom I discussed previously, were a part of my initial introduction to classical Japanese musical drama. I was invited by them (through Papa Tsugumo), to attend a Japanese play, a *Noh* drama, the title of which I do not recall. It was an unusual experience, and cleared up some of the mystery which I had written home to my family during the war from Ie Shima, when I said, "I cannot see how they [the Japanese] can stand that music night in and night out, for it is the most mournful music that one could ever hear. . . . It is very monotonous to us." The musical experience in Japan, through the tutelage of Papa Tsugumo, presented it in an entirely different light. Isn't it amazing how appreciative a person can be of anything when he understands it? The following is an account somewhat out of sequence from the previous monograph citation and describes my newly acquired appreciation for Japanese music:

> The Sunday following my last visit to the Japanese family for dinner in Ome, I was invited to attend a Japanese play, in which there was to be some of the finest dramatic talent in all of Japan. It was interesting to see how universal feelings are, and a knowledge of a language is not necessary to appreciate the thought behind the scene. At that time I practically knew none of the Japanese language. I had an interpreter . . . and really . . . I appreciated the play. This was my first introduction to the dramatic arts of Japan, and even though I forgot the name of the play, the players and the theme still linger in my memory. It was at this play that I [again] met [encountered] one of the greatest musicians in Japan, Professor G. Nakajima. He is a koto player. . . . After the play, we went to Professor Nakajima's home, which had been bombed and [almost] completely ruined. They now lived in a small cold two-roomed basement of the original house. It had been very elaborate and beautiful, as photographs showed. It was there that Miss Yasuko Nakajima played her koto. It was evident that music had been an inheritance from generations back. Miss Nakajima played a swift pleasant melody, which could not have been rendered by anyone, except a professional. Following this, she played a variation of Alexander's Rag Time Band. Miss Nakajima was, at that time, studying music in Tokyo. . . . The Nakajimas showed me a picture that they prize very greatly. It is a picture of Professor Nakajima, Yasha Heifits [Jascha Heifitz], and others. The picture was signed by Mr. Heifits. Professor Nakajima played a very difficult and famous composition for me. It was Rokudon. Later on Miss Nakajima played a descriptive composition about a mountain stream making its way down to the sea, named Seito ["Seioto"].

Totsuro Tsugumo, Taro Kikutani, and Mr. Date waiting for a train to visit the Toho Movie Studios.

Movies

I had seen a couple of Japanese movies, and was impressed with the surrealistic view of life which they presented. I should add, however, that not all their movies were surrealistic, for actually many were very realistic. Subsequently, Papa Tsugumo enabled me to visit a Japanese movie studio, as described in my monograph:

Papa Tsugumo invited me to an outing to a movie studio. Previous to this trip I had met a friend of his, Mr. Date, who was a dance instructor (instructor of the classical Japanese dance). He had previously worked for the studio, and it was through his efforts that we were permitted to visit the studio. We all met at the Tachikawa station, according to previous arrangements, and stopped at Mr. Tsugumo's home in Ichigoya for lunch. We then started out by train to visit the studio. We went back to Shinjuku, and took a small train, and after about an hour ride we left the train and started walking. This was still inside the city limits of Tokyo, I believe. The Toho Studios are located in between some hills, and it is a very large place. We were unable to see any shooting of scenes, because the workers were on strike, and were dramatically demonstrating. There were many people inside the compound, and they were all milling around. Of course they were striking for higher wages. Actually workers in the movie industry make very low wages, compared to other workers in Japan. I met several department heads, and several movie stars. Even though the workers were on strike we were taken on a tour of the plant. We were shown several sets. One was an English style hotel, with a very elaborate set. The other main set was a Japanese setting, which had been used for a gangster movie. I got some good photographs of the strike and the strikers. I had seen some Japanese movies before, when I went to the very unclean theater in Tachikawa. It was a war movie with good acting, but rather on the melodramatic side. In addition to the strike's preventing our viewing any shooting, there was another reason, namely that the troupe was on location at Kyoto.

Artwork

Papa Tsugumo always had time to explain to interested parties about the individual statues in his collection and to delve into the history behind them. In letters to my family and in my monograph, I discussed the collection of artwork which Papa Tsugumo had at his home in Ome.

His [Papa Tsugumo] home is beautiful and not too old, but it is patterned after a home that was styled centuries ago. One room is filled with statues and statuettes. He showed them all to me, and told me about them through an interpreter. He has the largest and most valuable of collections of its type in the world, many dating back to seven thousand years ago. . . .

My training in Oriental art began, really, when I first observed the art in Japanese homes, buildings, gardens, common utensils, clothing, etc. This accidental training was reinforced in some cases and refined in others through the personal attention of Papa Tsugumo. Some of the training was discussed in my monograph:

> One day I set out alone to Tokyo. I got off at Ichigoya, and with the aid of a policeman I was able to find the home of Papa Tsugumo. He had formerly had a huge house there, but it had been bombed out, and now all that remained was the storage vault, which he now used as his town house. Concrete vaults, such as this could be seen all over Japan. I do not know their specific purpose, but perhaps they were used to store food, grain and valuables. Mr. Tsugumo was now living in the one roomed vault, with an upper loft serving as a bedroom. There had been a hastily built room that was used for the kitchen, and the maid's quarters which was next to the vault. Mr. Tsugumo's son and daughter [Totsurosan] were living with him here, for they were both going to a middle school in Tokyo.
>
> In my many visits to Papa Tsugumo's home in Ome, I had occasion to examine his antiques and curios. He got me interested in them, and he told me to come to Tokyo some day, and we would go shopping for them in a certain section of Tokyo. He said he would show me how to discern the good genuine articles from the facsimiles and imitations. It was a wonderful opportunity to learn something about Oriental art.
>
> When I later returned to Tokyo to visit the shops, we walked from Papa Tsugumo's home in Ichigoya. As we were walking down a side road, Papa Tsugumo pointed out to me the homes of several princes and generals. Many of them had been bombed, but several of them remained intact. I remember one in particular, and I took a picture of it, calling it, "*Kojo no Tsuke*" (that is a song title which means "Moonlight on the Deserted Castle," and the song was very popular in Japan). We went to a subway station and waited for the train. . . .
>
> Papa Tsugumo and I finally arrived at our destination, and proceeded to inspect the shops. I looked at several things, and many of the things that I picked up, appraised their age, country, and value were wrong. He would then explain how to tell the difference. We came to one shop, and I saw an unique dish. I stopped to look at it. It was in the window, and Papa Tsugumo said it could not be any good, or they would not be selling it that low. I remember the price was 70 yen, which at that time was about $4.34. We went in and Papa Tsugumo examined the dish. He said that it was much more valuable than that, for it was one of the originals of the Kutani Company. It was about 350 years old, or perhaps older. He said that he would buy it. He talked with the shopkeeper for awhile. I expected him to bargain with

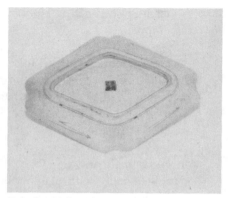

Original Kutani-ware bowl Papa Tsugumo and I found in a Tokyo shop.

Kutani-ware bowl (reverse side).

Korean ceramic bowl, 1,000 years old (can be used for special celebrations such as the tea ceremony).

The Kutani wine cup with poem inscribed inside, of which there were only four in existence (three were given to American officers and one was retained by Papa Tsugumo in Miyanohira).

the shopkeeper, but he didn't. He bought it but paid them more than they asked, for he felt it would not be honest to buy it at the price they set. I had been accustomed to bargaining with the Japanese before buying anything, for I could usually get it cheaper. In the same shop he examined a small incense burner, and I was surprised at him when he bought it. I asked him if it were valuable. He said, "No, it is a new thing, but it is nicely designed and I like it." Since then I deducted [sic] that the thing that he originally bought, the dish, was much more valuable than he paid for it so he bought the incense burner to soothe his conscience. This shows how honest the Japanese can be about things.

As I was leaving his home in Ichigoya, he presented me with the dish that I had located and that he bought. I was surprised and declined, but he insisted, stating that it was rightfully mine, and that he wanted to give it to me anyhow. At the same time he also presented me with a tea bowl from Korea that was 1,000 years old. Additionally he gave me a sugar bowl that was 100 years old. It was a beautiful thing decorated in red, white and green. It was Rokuby ware, and came from southern Japan.

In his home in Miyanohira, Papa Tsugumo showed us a room with perhaps hundreds of statues (primarily Buddhist) which had been taken there for safekeeping during the war. I have reason to believe from our conversations that some of the statues stored there may have been from the Imperial Castle. The vista was extremely impressive, and a view I will never forget. Many of the statues were thousands of years old (in 1960 it was stated that he had 3,500, with one being 1,600 years old). We did not examine them closely, but rather from the open sliding door of the room. I was so awe-struck that I just stood there and did not even attempt to walk into the crowded room.

Papa Tsugumo had presented me with very many art treasures, many of which are priceless. I still have most of them on display in my home to enjoy and admire. Some of these art treasures have been mentioned, such as the small wooden figurine of Bisha Mon, God of War, which was around 350 years old at that time. The Korean bowl used in the tea ceremony was 1,000 years old. There is also an ancient Hari-kari knife and a handsome wooden lacquered sheath, with a finely balanced throwing knife slid into the sheath. I do not know its age, but it is obviously very old (probably around 350 years), as can be observed from the inscription on the blade. Papa Tsugumo also presented me with a black lacquered vase (5½" x 14") with a golden dragon winding around the vase. Two other items were incense boxes, one in red lacquer with a dragon carved on the lid, and another of very old porcelain with a butterfly crest (the crest of the House of Tsugumo). That porcelain box still contains some very old incense which was inside when he presented it to me.

Papa Tsugumo on Christmas Day 1945 showed me a relic which was about 400 years old. It was a sort of stool made of copper or bronze, with a crucifix molded into its top. Christianity was banned in Japan at that former time. This stool, called a "stepping stool," was used as a test to determine whether or not a person was a Christian. A person was asked to step on the crucifix, and if he did not he was considered to be a Christian and was killed.

There are also several Japanese prints, Papa Tsugumo gave me. I do not know all their origins, but I do know about some of them, which have been identified by several Japanese visitors and from having taken colored photographs to the Boston Museum of Art. I know that the prints are genuine, and I treasure them greatly (in 1960 he estimated that 80 percent of the woodblock prints acquired by outsiders and claimed as originals were not originals). The works he presented to me include two brilliantly colored single-panel prints — apparently Tsukoka Ko-Jio, "*Hagoromo*" two of the 100 *Noh* Drama Scenes, Meiji, nineteenth century. (A print identical to one of mine appeared on the cover of the Fall/Winter 1989 catalog from Indiana University Press.)

There are also five three-panel prints. One is of the Imperial Castle, Meiji 21st year, by Kiei (b. 1888). Another is apparently of the first Sino-Japanese War (1894-1895); it is in very somber tones and shows the well-armed and well-equipped victorious Japanese advancing on an ill-equipped, pig-tailed Chinese army.

One print is of a Kabuki theatre drama, which I understand carries the name of an artist, Ichiyusai Kokuho. I do not know the age of the print, but it appears to be somewhere near that of another print (in both cases blue tones predominate), a Samurai family (nobility) checking out its wardrobe. The latter is apparently by Toyokuni (1769-1825). Basil Stewart (*A Guide to Japanese Prints and Their Subject Matter*) indicates that Toyokuni was a pupil of Toyoharu and was also the most prominent artist of the Utagawa School. He was a prolific high-quality artist and specialized in creating portraits of actors and figure studies. He appeared, also, to have had many students.

"Beauty in Twelve Months" is the title of a series of prints by Shuntei (1770-1820), one of which Papa Tsugumo gave me, and I would assume that it was given to me during the period covered in the print, namely October. Another one is a single panel of a classical Japanese girl with a goldfish in a bowl, called "Beauty of Gay Circle," apparently by Choshosai.

I also received two small paintings, one on silk and one on silver leaf, for which I do not know the history, but I would assume that the one on silk of delicate poppies is contemporary. The other one on silver leaf appears to be much older, and it appears that some of the tempera-colored parts were retouched.

Other items include a statuette made of bamboo humorously showing a man yawning with outstretched arms. Another is very small and of extremely hard wood, with two monkeys fighting over an orange (*mekang*). Mama Tsugumo gave me a set of modern "his and hers" teacups with covers, sans handles. I believe they are modern Kutani. I have perhaps mentioned already that Papa Tsugumo had four small, antique Kutani wine cups with poems inscribed inside, of which he gave one to me, one to Father Joynt (the Catholic chaplain), probably one to Lieutenant Stoney, and one he kept himself. He indicated that every time we took a sip from our cups we would remember the others (the cup I have became damaged during one of my many moves, but I still have most of

Fish hatchery near Papa Tsugumo's mountain retreat at Miyanohira.

the pieces). A red lacquer saki cup with the Tokugawa crest was another gift, but I cannot locate it anymore. Mama Tsugumo gave me a needlework she created herself, showing a Japanese garden scene. It is finely made with a number of different stitches and different yarns and threads, on black silk, and is always admired. I also have a beautifully gray-shaded jade cup with variegated light-brown coloring and a small dark spot or two, finely crafted, which is about three inches high and about two inches wide at the top, given to me by Papa Tsugumo.

Fishing

Fish are an important part of the life of the Japanese people, from the tiniest which can hardly be seen, to the giant whales. Their flesh was (and I presume still is) the staple of the Japanese diet. I had been invited to Papa Tsugumo's mountain retreat at Miyanohira a number of times. It was the locale of a fishing "expedition" for a group of us. There was a very cold, fast-moving stream that went by the retreat. When I once asked if there were any fish in the stream, I was advised that it was so fast-moving that there were only very small fish at that time of year. Sometime later, when we visited there we went "fishing." This involved using extremely beautiful sectional bamboo poles with the thinnest of silk lines and a hook one could hardly see. Bait was not used, but instead, the line was flung upstream and was followed downstream, wiggling it from side to side. Usually there was nothing on the hook, but once in awhile a prize was landed. The fish were about two inches long, and almost transparent, with an orange hue. After enough of these "beauties" were caught, they were immediately dipped into batter and fried, insides and all. At first, it was a little difficult to eat them, but later, when you forgot the foregoing, they tasted great.

This fishing experience led to another one which had a surprising ending for us, as I indicated in the monograph.

It was after I asked about the fish that he [Papa Tsugumo] invited me to come up to visit a friend of his who lived near a place where there were plenty of trout. He told me to bring a friend along. Father Joynt, the Catholic Chaplain, and Lt. Hect, the Mess officer, joined me for the visit. We took two jeeps, and went to Ome. We went inside and had tea, and were introduced to Papa Tsugumo's friends. Then we headed for the mountains. We packed the jeeps with the family. It was pre-arranged that the mayor of the village at our destination would have our fishing tackle and everything prepared. When we arrived the mayor hadn't arrived, so we waited for him. Finally we ate a small lunch, after we entered the newly built home. It was a beautiful place built upon stilts on the mountain side. From the huge windows one could look down over the mountainous landscape.

We found out why this was a good place for trout, for just below the house was a fish hatchery. Below the hatchery was a pond with huge black fish swimming around. The standing joke between us Americans was that the Japanese didn't want to make us feel bad because we couldn't catch any fish, so they brought us to a place where we couldn't miss.

Part of our meal that day consisted of canned salmon, candied beef, and smoked trout. Part of the reason for our unusual meal was that our host, the mayor, never arrived [with other parts of our meal]. We finally started back in the jeeps. As we were turning out into the main road, we saw the mayor. He was on his bicycle and held the fishing equipment. We stopped and Papa Tsugumo talked to him rather

Tarosan at Papa Tsugumo's town house in Ichigaya.

excitedly. We went back, never having gone fishing. So, even though we were in a fish hatchery, we didn't catch any fish.

History

Papa Tsugumo often discussed the history of Japan. Although he did so, I

Mama Tsugumo beside the Christmas tree of bamboo and pine decorated with cotton and carrying a banner saying "Merry Xmas & Welcome Bob" at Ome.

am afraid that my recollections are rather dim, unfortunately. He described the time he spent in China, Korea, and other places. It was during one of these conversations he presented me with the Japanese print, illustrating the first Sino-Japanese War which had occurred from 1894-1895.

In his discussions, Papa Tsugumo, always related history to art (or was it art to history?). He illustrated the introduction of specific art form and design from China to Korea, and then from Korea to Japan. He also indicated that there appeared to be some Semitic influences in Korean and Japanese art. He further indicated that, accordingly, there appeared to be some reason to believe that the Japanese (and apparently the Koreans) may have been Semitic in origin. In fact, he said that they themselves may even have been from one of the lost tribes of Israel. Actually, some Japanese do appear to have Semitic features.

Other Events

Before concluding this chapter of my life with the House of Tsugumo, I should relate events which I have not divulged to anyone before, but which should be told to complete the account.

Once when I was alone and while changing trains going from Ome to Tachikawa, I had a gift from Papa Tsugumo wrapped in a cloth napkin (used to wrap gifts), with his name on it (as I recall, it was purple). A Japanese youth came up to me at the train station and in English made a derogatory remark about Papa Tsugumo, saying that he was a part of the military and should be treated as other military people who were under investigation. I admonished the person with a statement that "the war was not against an individual, but rather against the people of an entire nation." I did nothing further with the information from that youth.

In discussions with Papa Tsugumo, it became clear that his role in the war appeared to be that of an advisor and a member of the House of Peers, not necessarily a military advisor, although he apparently had been a General. Information from Japan at a much later date indicated that Papa Tsugumo had been absolved of any connection with other military or political wrongdoing during World War II.

On another occasion, while traveling in either Hachioji, Hino, or Tachikawa, another Japanese youth approached me and pointed out a house which he said contained many priceless antiques, relics, and other precious things which had been stolen during the war. I really do not know what he expected me to do, for I would imagine the homes of any one in the upper echelon of society may have had objects with similar origins. I considered it merely an allegation, not necessarily a fact. I did not mention this to anyone, either.

A lesson in a part of the niceties of the Japanese language was clearly brought out to me when I was walking in Ichigoya with Papa Tsugumo. The area around Ichigoya had been heavily bombed. Walking through the rubble-strewn area was hazardous for one had to step over stones, boulders, broken concrete, potholes, etc., with few regular sidewalks remaining. That area really "caught it." As I recall, Papa Tsugumo and I were returning at dusk on a dark, rainy afternoon from visiting the Nakajima's house (also in Ichigoya). As we were walking, I saw a mud puddle and a protruding piece of concrete. I didn't think Papa Tsugumo saw it, so I called out loudly and quickly, "*KIOTSKE!*" I understood that the word meant "be careful," or "stop." Papa Tsugumo unhesitatingly stopped abruptly. He turned to me and asked what

Mama Tsugumo, Taro Kikutani, and Tirosan at Christmas dinner at Ome.

was the matter. I explained. Then he said, "Do you know what you just said?"
I indicated I did and that it meant "be careful" or "stop." He said "You are
right, it does mean 'stop,' but it is a military command." He indicated that
when using that word, one should add some ending to it. He suggested that I

use *"Kiotske na sai."* I found one could soften other words by adding *"na sai."*

Personal Notes

I occasionally hear from "The House of Tsugumo." It is always from my Japanese brother, Taro Kikutani, Papa Tsugumo's son-in-law, husband of his oldest daughter, Namikosan. Namikosan lived with her mother as long as her mother was alive. I correspond occasionally and usually send Christmas cards, and they usually reply. I recently spoke to them by phone, but alas, I was saddened because my Japanese was so poor that I was unable to communicate effectively.

In one letter, I was pleased to learn that the Tsugumos and the Kikutanis had not forgotten me. Mama Tsugumo, according to her son-in-law, used to say, "Bob is my son of America." In that same letter, I was surprised to learn that Tarosan's wife, Namikosan, stated that "Bob was very gentle." I was surprised, for I had never considered myself gentle, but I was pleased that the Tsugumo family felt that way about me. Tarosan also discussed the Christmas dinner which we had so long ago in her letter to me of January 1970:

> Every Christmas time I remember that we celebrated the first Christmas for you in Japan. We didn't have a Christmas tree, so we used a pine tree, bamboo and cotton from our garden. That was a completely Japanese style Christmas. Do you remember? It seems like just last year. We hung up a banner of paper on that tree which said, "Merry Christmas and Welcome Bob." My son is already the same age that you were at that time.

In Retrospect

In retrospect, I am continually amazed that the House of Tsugumo, relatives, and friends were able to — and actually did — devote so much time, expense, and attention to me, a relatively unimportant junior officer in the Occupation force. I am certain now that I must have been a terrible imposition to them, a great source of inconvenience, and perhaps even an embarrassment at times. However, they never let me feel that. It is only now that I realize that this must have been the case. It is also now that I acknowledge that the feeling of Ohn has been with me all my life since my stay in Japan. This volume is one small attempt to relieve me of some of the burdens and obligations of Ohn under which I have lived throughout the years (although its effects were ameliorated by the fact that they considered me part of their family).

Chapter 7

Return to the United States

Oh, say can you see, by the dawn's early light.

Francis Scott Key,
The Star Spangled Banner

The Voyage Home

The day of departure finally arrived, 14 July 1946. I had previously shipped back a considerable number of packages. The balance of my precious possessions and my clothing needed for the return were packed in duffle bags, of which we were permitted two. The waiting around became endless, especially the wait to board the ungainly *Marshall Victory,* a slow, barely seaworthy "victory ship." I was advised that the hull of this ship was constructed of concrete, and it was anything but a cruise ship, either in looks, performance, or accommodations.

Our route back was the great circle from Tokyo to Seattle, Washington. As such, we passed close to Alaska and, in fact, could see its shores from the ship. The weather was incredibly inclement, adding to the natural discomfort of the ship, and almost everyone aboard got sick. They didn't leave their bunks, and, mind you, we were stacked in cloth bunks which were at least three or four high. Because of the bad weather, and other people's seasickness, I did not spend any more time there than absolutely necessary. I certainly did not have much competition in the mess hall. Whenever I went in, the personnel would wait on me as if I were at the Waldorf. They would encourage me to eat — specially prepared steak, special dishes, and, *particularly*, the desserts they had prepared. I gained some weight on the way back (but still only weighed about 135 pounds).

The Victory ship, *Marshall Victory*, which brought Flight Officer Vaughn and other troops back from Japan on 14 July 1946.

It was a glorious sight on 24 July 1946 to see Seattle coming into view, closer and closer. As we approached the pier, there was a tug which came alongside with an orchestra and singers and a huge sign reading "Welcome Home." It was an exciting and glorious change from much that had preceded.

Seattle, Washington, welcome-home celebration.

Ft. Sheridan, Illinois

From Seattle, we traveled by train to Ft. Sheridan, Illinois, where we were processed for separation. Officers were not given Honorable Discharges in

Army of the United States

Honorable Discharge

This is to certify that

ROBERT V. VAUGHN

15_____, Aviation Cadet, Section "H", AAFBU

Army of the United States

is hereby Honorably Discharged from the military service of the United States of America.

This certificate is awarded as a testimonial of Honest and Faithful Service to his country.

Given at AAFFS (A-__), Moody Field, Georgia

Date 7 September 1944

For the Commanding Officer:

LEWIS H. KENSINGER,
Lt. Col., Air Corps,
Deputy for Adm & Services.

W. D., A. G. O. Form No. 55
January 22, 1943

OHIO WORLD WAR II | CLAIM
COMPENSATION APPLIED FOR | NO.   487134

Honorable Discharge, A/C Vaughn, 7 September 1944.

Army of the United States

CERTIFICATE OF SERVICE

This is to certify that

ROBERT V VAUGHN   T 65 915   F/O

317th Troop Carrier Group

honorably served in active Federal Service

in the Army of the United States from

8 September 1944   *to*   20 September 1946

Given at   SEPARATION CENTER   Fort Sheridan Illinois

on the   20th   *day of*   September   *19* 46

J. A. CARROLL
MAJ. CAV.

Military Record and Report of Separation, Flight Officer Vaughn, 20 September 1946.

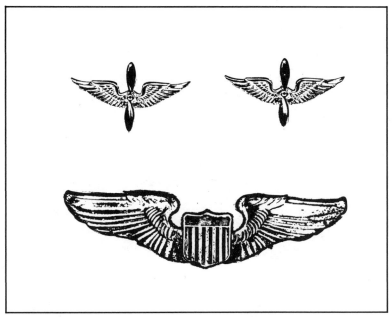

Flight Officer Vaughn's original USAAF Pilot wings and Air Force insignia.

those days, but instead were given a "Certificate of Service," which included the "Military Record and Report of Separation." This was given to Flight Officers as well as to Lieutenants and higher officers, even though the separation of the Flight Officers was actually a discharge, because the position of Flight Officer was discontinued and no longer used. As previously stated, the Army was trying to change the Flight Officers into Second Lieutenants, apparently so that they could be retained in the Army Air Forces Reserve (as such, they could have been called up for Korea, Vietnam, etc.).

Terminal Leave

I was on terminal leave from 29 July 1946 through 20 September 1946. I visited relatives in Chicago, as I was nearby at Ft. Sheridan, and then traveled to my home in Carey, Ohio. My career in the military service ended on 20 September 1946.

Epilogue

Have you forgotten yet? . . .
Look up and swear by the slain of the war that you'll never forget.

Sigfried Sassoon,
The Aftermath

At my present age, I have a view of the world tempered by military service in World War II, by Occupation duty in Japan, by studies leading to a B.S., B.A., M.A., and an Ed.D., and by having reflected on my early experiences and writings. I now have a better grasp of the psychological effects which others had on me, and which I had on others during the short time frame of the four years covered in this volume. Some of these effects are assumed on my part. Although there are many suppositions and assumptions in this narrative, I have tried to be factual and to not fantasize. There may be some distortion of facts or events, however, they are not intentional, and your forbearance is solicited. In all cases, I have intended to be sympathetic to all parties. During the war we never heard the word "Japanese," but rather "Jap." As a result, my early writings reflected the latter word. In this narrative, however, I have replaced "Jap" with "Japanese."

World War II was sometimes called a war to defend democracy. One has to wonder whether democracy was defended when there were created two Berlins, two Germanys, and one larger expanded USSR after the war. This is especially questionable because now many areas of the USSR, which were taken over by the Soviets, have revolted either for separation or independence. And this from one of our Allies who, theoretically at least, was also fighting a

war to defend democracy. We who fought in World War II called it "The War."
The Russians called it "The Great Patriotic War." Whatever it was, the results
were not what any of the parties expected. Much of the rancor and distrust of
the Russians has disintegrated since then. Even now we have cooperative
ventures with them economically, politically, and militarily (in relation to the
Gulf-Iraqi crisis).

While I may not have had a great influence on the outcome of World War II,
nor of the resurgence of the Japanese nation, they have had a great influence
upon me. I have already noted the effect that the Occupation experience had
on my later life, having instilled in me a love of language, and of peoples, their
customs, and their arts.

Flying and Aircraft

I loved aviation and dreamed of flying long before entering military service.
I designed, constructed, and flew model airplanes. To this very day, I avidly
follow aviation and astronautics. I enjoyed learning to fly. I was never more
happy at that youthful time than when I was flying.

After completing training, I had hoped to be assigned to more exotic
aircraft, such as P-51 Mustangs, P-38 Lightnings, A-20 Havocs, P-63 King
Cobras, and even B-26 Marauders. Such was not the case. Instead, I was
assigned to B-24 Liberators, and, later on, to C-46 Commandos.

The B-24 was a huge aircraft which required considerable strength to fly
(particularly when trying to make a tight turn). In rough weather, it took a
tremendous effort to keep it level and on course. I was only 5-foot, 6-inches
and weighed about 130 pounds. As such, this was a difficult plane for me to fly.
The same was to a lesser extent true for the C-46, although it was not really an
easy plane to fly, either.

I should add that while I did not particularly enjoy flying the two
aforementioned aircraft, I appreciated their capabilities and what I felt was
their safety. I had seen B-24s lose perhaps six or eight feet of a wing tip or lose
half of their elevators and one stabilizer and still land safely. I saw C-46s
floating in the sea, long after they had been ditched. Those experiences gave
me confidence in flying them. I loved flying then, and still enjoy seeing others
fly the aircraft which I never had the opportunity to pilot, or for which I was
much too old.

One of the things which is rarely thought of, much less spoken about, is that
some pilots are very superstitious. One of the superstitions hinted at is the
matter of "luck running out." I guess to some extent, I felt that way after I was
discharged from military service. I always passed off not flying by indicating
humorously that "the world below was better off since I gave up flying."

The Japanese People

It became evident to me that the Japanese people were more than helpful immediately after the war in preventing further tensions. They were, in fact, eager to assist in teaching their culture and history to the newcomers who knew nothing about them. The fact that so many Japanese actually spoke English at a time like that (and so few Americans spoke Japanese) proved that they were very adaptive and could accommodate diversity. The actual warm interpersonal relationships which developed after the war, while remaining relatively inactive for years, still remain imbedded in my memory. If they remain for me, then most certainly they must for many of my contemporaries, not to mention the thousands of Americans who have been to Japan for travel, employment, military service, etc., since that time over 40 years ago. My brother, James Vaughn, also was stationed in Japan for many years, long after my departure, and, in fact, his two children went to high school there. He and his family have very deep personal regard for the Japanese people and their culture, which have influenced all four of their lives.

I anticipate that although modern adversities may develop over the years between the Japanese and the Americans, they will be moderated by the memories of those who were fortunate enough to have been in Japan in the early years, but who also were fortunate enough to have been accepted into a family of the Japanese people.

Atomic and Nuclear Bombs

World War I taught us that we could not use poison gas as a weapon. World War II taught us that atomic or nuclear bombs cannot be used as weapons, either aggressively or defensively. Tragic as the use of the A-bombs on Hiroshima and Nagasaki were, they permitted ending a bloody war, and demonstrated to the world that atomic or nuclear bombs could not be used in the future. Although the presence of those weapons still exists, it is doubtful that any "responsible" party would use them. There is always, however, the potential for them to be abused by extremists and their governments (such as perhaps exists in the present Gulf crisis). Hopefully, the lessons of World War II will remain uppermost.

Select Bibliography

Birdsall, Steve, *The Log of the Liberators* (Garden City, NY: Doubleday and Co., 1973).

Blattau, Philip J., "Articles like These Strain My Loyalty," *The Catholic Review,* MD: Baltimore (22 Aug. 1990), 8.

Blow, Michael, *The History of the Atomic Bomb* (New York: American Heritage Publishing Co., Inc., 1968).

Board of Tourist Industry, *Nippon* (Tokyo: Japanese Government Railways, n.d. [pre-war]).

Board of Tourist Industry, *Pocket Guide to Japan* (Tokyo: Japanese Government Railways, 1939).

Board of Tourist Industry, *Souvenirs: What and Where* (Tokyo: Japanese Government Railways, n.d. [pre-war]).

Boeman, John, *Morotai: A Memoir of War,* rev. ed. (Manhattan, KS: Sunflower University Press, 1989).

Boorstein, Daniel J., "Political Technology," *Harper's* (Mar. 1978), 43-50.

Bowie, Henry P., *On the Laws of Japanese Painting* (1911; New York: Dover Publications, n.d.).

Busch, Noel F., *The Horizon Concise History of Japan* (New York: American Heritage Publishing Co., Inc., 1972).

Carigan, William, *Ad Lib: Flying the B-24 Liberator in World War II* (Manhattan, KS: Sunflower University Press, 1988).

Cavey, James T., "There is no Guilt on My Part," *The Catholic Review* (22 Aug. 1990), 8.

Craig, William, *The Fall of Japan* (New York: Dial Press, 1967).

Cubbins, William R., *The War of the Cotton-Tails: Memoirs of a WWII Bomber Pilot* (Chapel Hill, NC: Algonquin Books of Chapel Hill, *c.* 1989).

Darr Aero Tech, *The B.T.O. 44-H* (Albany, GA: Darr Aero Tech, [1944]).

Del Tredici, *At Work in the Fields of the Bomb* (New York: Harper & Row, 1987).

Duncan, Robert L., *The Day the Sun Fell* (New York: Pinnacle Books, 1970).

Feinsilber, Mike, "Data Shows Japan Mulled Counter A-Bomb," *San Juan Star*, 29 May 1978, 10.

General Dynamics Convair Division, *Liberator* (St. Louis, MO: General Dynamics Corp., 1989).

Goralski, Robert, *World War II Almanac: 1931-1945* (New York: G.P. Putnam's Sons, 1981).

Greenfield, John, "That Bomb Was No Sin," *The Catholic Review* (22 Aug. 1990), 8.

Harris, Jonathon, *Hiroshima, A Study in Science, Politics, and the Ethics of War* (Amherst Project Committee on the Study of History) (Menlo, CA: Addison-Wesley Publishing Co., 1970).

Hartman, William H., "When the Japanese Repent, I Might," *The Catholic Review* (22 Aug. 1990), 8.

Henle, Fritz, *Das Ist Japan* (Bad Hartzburg: Dr. Walther Herring Verlag, 1937).

Hersey, John, *Hiroshima* (New York: Alfred A. Knopf, 1946).

Hughes, Robert, "The Art of the Japanese Sword," *Horizon Magazine* (Mar. 1979), 50-60.

International B-24 Liberator Club [San Diego, CA], *Briefing, Special Edition, 1990*.

Kindaiti, Kyosuke, *Ainu Life and Legend* (Tokyo: Japanese Government Railways, 1941).

Leckie, Robert, *Delivered from Evil: The Saga of World War II,* Perennial Library (New York: Harper & Row, 1987).

MacWilliams, J. H. and Callander, Bruce D., "The Third Lieutenants," *Air Force Magazine* (Mar. 1990), 100-102.

Martin, John G., *It Began at Imphal: The Combat Cargo Story* (Manhattan, KS: Sunflower University Press, 1988).

Metropolitan Museum of Art, *A Guide to the Collections, Part 1, Ancient and Oriental Art* (New York: Metropolitan Museum of Art, 1937).

Midzukami, Hitoshi, *A Collection of Japanese Proverbs and Sayings* (Tokyo: Kairyudo Press, 1940).

Nakamura, Tanio, *Contemporary Japanese-style Painting* (New York: Tudor Publishing Co., 1969).

Okada, Yuzuri, *Japanese Family Crests* (Tokyo: Japanese Government Railways, 1941).

Prange, Gordon W., *At Dawn We Slept* (New York: McGraw Hill, 1981).

Prange, Gordon W., Goldstein, Donald M., and Dillon, Katherine V., *Dec. 7,*

1941: The Day the Japanese Attacked Pearl Harbor (New York: Warner Books, 1988).

Rosenbaum, Ron, "The Subterranean World of the Bomb." *Harper's* (Mar. 1978), 85-108.

Sarasota [FL] Herald-Tribune, "Japan Observes Anniversary of Bomb Blast," 6 Aug. 1978, 5-A.

Shattuck, Lewis A., "Masterpieces from Japan's Past," *Pacific Stars and Stripes* (Tokyo: Troop Information and Education Section, HQ, Far East Command, [exact date unknown] 1960), 15.

Silverman, William A., "The Plot to Stop the Emperor's Surrender," Detroit, MI: *Sunday Magazine* (7 Feb. 1971), 43-52.

Southeast Army Air Force Training Center, *Maxwell Field, Alabama: Headquarters S.E.A.A.F. Training Center* (Montgomery, AL: SAAF, n.d).

Stewart, Basil, *A Guide to Japanese Prints and Their Subject Matter* (New York: Dover Publications Inc., 1979).

Toland, John, *The Rising Sun: The Decline and Fall of the Japanese Empire, 1936-1945* (New York: Random House, 1970).

Trimbull, Tanio, "Veterans Ask Japan to Restore Status of Shrine to War Dead," *The New York Times,* 16 Aug. 1973, 4.

Vaccari, Oreste, and Vaccari, Enko Elisa, *The Up-to-date English-Japanese Conversation Dictionary,* 10th ed. (Rutland, VT: Charles E. Tuttle Co., 1954).

Vaughn, Robert V., *An American Airman's Experiences in Post-war Japan (1945-1946)* (Christiansted, St. Croix, VI: By the Author, 1969).

Vaughn, Robert V., "My Life in the Service: The diary of Robert V. Vaughn," 8 Apr. 1943-16 June 1945.

Warner, Langdon, *The Enduring Art of Japan* (New York: Grove Press, 1952).

Publications

by Robert V. Vaughn

An Almanac for St. Thomas Airport Planners (Christiansted, VI: Aye Aye Press, 1974)

Another Search: Dissertations Accepted at the University of Sarasota 1971 (Christiansted, VI: Aye Aye Press, January 1979)

"Automation of Bibliographic Services in the Caribbean: Two Cases in the United States Virgin Islands." Paper presented before the Association of Caribbean University and Research Institutions Libraries (ACURIL), Trinidad, May 1984

"CD-ROM in Small Libraries: Its Present and Its Future," *CMC News* (Cannon Falls, MN) (Spring 1989)

Creole Studies — A Conference on Theoretical Orientation. Post-conference source book of the College of Virgin Islands (Christiansted, VI: Aye Aye Press, 1979)

Local Government vs. Centralized Government in the U.S. Virgin Islands (Christiansted, VI: Aye Aye Press, 1977)

Using Computers in the Classroom Teaching Process (Christiansted, VI: Aye Aye Press, 1982)

The Air Transport Industry Serving the Virgin Islands and the West Indies (Christiansted, VI: Aye Aye Press, 1975)

The Cheap Shot (Christiansted, VI: Aye Aye Press, 1980; space/espionage fiction)

The Development of a Dictionary of Selected Words and Phrases of the Creole Language as Spoken by the People of St. Lucia, Ph.D. dis., University of Sarasota (FL), 1979

The Virgin Islands Pre-White House Conference on Library and Information

Services, a Source Book (Christiansted, VI: Aye Aye Press, 1979)

To St. Lucia with Love (Christiansted, VI: Aye Aye Press, 1980; bibliography)

Virgin Islands Acronyms (Christiansted, VI: Aye Aye Press, 1987)

Virgin Islands Business Journal Index (Christiansted, VI: Aye Aye Press, 1989; computer data base)

"Virgin Islands Mass Communications 1981 — A Survey." Paper presented at the Caribbean Studies Association, St. Thomas, May 1981.

Virgin Islands Newspapers — Substantive Index (Christiansted, VI: Aye Aye Press, 1982-1989; computer data base)

Virgin Islands of the United States: Social, Economic, and Political Conditions Referred to in Recent Periodical Literature (Christiansted, VI: Aye Aye Press, 1974)

Whither "CD-ROM (Under OS/2)?" *CD-ROM Librarian* (Apr. 1989)

Index

Compiled by Lori L. Daniel

— A —

AAA (anti-aircraft battery), 38-39
Africa, 1
Aftermath, The, 1
Aircraft
  A-20 Havocs, 167
  AT-10, xii, 4, 18-20
  B-17, 1
  B-24 liberator Bomber, xii, 1, 25, 29, 32-33,
    38, 40-44, 67, 87, 167
  B-25, 52
  B-26 Marauders, 167
  B-29, 33, 43, 48-50, 52, 87
  B-32, 33-35, 43
  BT-13 Vultee Valiant (Vultee Vibrator), xii, 4,
    17-19
  C-46 Curtis Commando (The Whale), 29, 38,
    57, 61-65, 67, 69-70, 79, 167
  C-47, 57
  C-54 Skymaster, 26-27, 36, 52, 56-57
  Northrop P-61 Black Widow, 38-39
  P-38 lightning, 32, 37-38, 52, 167
  P-39 Airacobra, 17-25
  P-51 Mustang, 63, 167
  P-63 Kingcobra, 25, 167
  Piper Cub, 10
  PT-13 Stearman (Boeing Kaydet), 4, 11, 13,
    17-18
Air Force Magazine, 20, 22
Alabama
  Maxwell Field, 4, 11-12
Alaska, 160
Allies, 27, 45, 48, 166
American (Cano), 31-32, 43, 48-49, 52-53, 71,
  74, 77, 90-91, 110, 112, 114, 116, 131-133, 136,
  140-144, 150, 154, 159, 168
  Indian, 1

*American Airman's Experiences in Post-War Ja-
  pan (1945-1946), An*, x, 61
Andrews Sisters, 5
Angur Island, 69
Arab-Israeli conflict, 46
Armistice Day, *see* Veteran's Day
Asia, 25
Asiatic/Pacific war zone, ix
Atlantic Ocean, 25
Atomic bomb, ix, 33, 43-49, 168
  Fat Man, ix
  Super bomb, 43, 48
Australia, 38, 67
Aviation Cadet, 3, 19
  training, ix
Axis, 25

— B —

Back to Bataan, 30
Baker, Navigator Second Lieutenant Fred E., 29
Baron, Margie, xvii, 1
Bato, Michigi, 105-106
Beech aircraft, xii, 4, 18, 20
Bell Aircraft, 17, 25
Bermuda Triangle, 25
Bernoulli effect, 62
Betty bomber, *see* Japanese airplane
Bisha Mon (God of War), 131, 134-135, 151
Black market, xii, 94, 106
Blue pickle, 21, 23
Boano, Father, 99, 102
Boeing, 4, 13
Bomb
  Atomic, *see* Atomic bomb
  Nuclear, *see* Nuclear bomb
  Paper, *see* Paper Bomb
  Super, *see* Atomic bomb

Bombay, xv
British, 52
Buddha, 111, 130
Buddhist, 78, 101, 108, 151
Burma, 131
Butsuzo-no-ma, 129

— C —

California, ix
  Hamilton Field, ix, 26-27
  Salinas, 25
  San Francisco, 25-26
    Golden Gate, 26
    Top of the Mark, 26
Callander, Bruce D., 20, 23
Cargo Transport, 57
Caribbean, x, 117
Catholic, 99, 101, 152, 154
Chiesa, Father, 99-102
China, 67, 108, 119, 131, 156
  Seas, xv
  Shanghai, xv
Chinese, xv, 52, 152
Christian, 78, 151
Civil War, 6
Colombo, xv
Columbia University, 102
Conte Verde, xv
Craig, William, 45
C-Rations, 70
Curtis, Flight Officer Elmo, 34, 65, 96

— D —

Das Ist Japan, x, 89
Date, Mr., 147
Desert Storm Gulf war, 46

— E —

Eastern Flying Training Command, 10
Elman, Mischa, 145
England, 1
English, 78, 82, 88, 90, 104-105, 108, 116, 118,
  127-128, 133-135, 144, 148, 157, 168
Europe, 1, 16, 18, 25

— F —

Fall of Japan, The, 45
Fifth Air Force, 29
  43rd Bomb Group, 23, 29, 32, 58
Filipinos, 30-31
Fisher, Lieutenant, 96-97
Fish hatchery, 153-155
Florida, 20
  Miami, 6, 10
  Miami Beach, 3, 6-7
    Hotel Biarritz, 6-7
    Hotel National, 6
  Okefenokee Swamp, 20
  Panama City, 25
    Tyndal Field, 25

France, 101
French, 102, 117, 133
Fujisan, *see* Mount Fuji
Fujita, H., 106
Fujiyama, *see* Mount Fuji

— G —

Geisha, 78
  girls, 82
  house, 80-81
General Dynamics, xii
Georgia, 20
  Albany, 4, 11-12, 15-16
    Darr Aero Tech, 4, 11-12, 15-16
  Augusta, 4, 17-18
    Bush Field, 4
  Valdosta, 18
    Moody Field, 4, 18, 20
German, 133
Germany, 101, 166
  Berlin, 166
  Regensburg, 16
Getas (platform wooden shoes), 85
Good Hope School, xi
Gook, *see* Japaneses
Guam, 27, 69
Gulf-Iraqi crisis, 167-168

— H —

Hari-kari knife, 151
Harper's Bazaar, x
Hashi (chopsticks), 131, 133
Hawaii, 27
  Hickam Field, 27
  Pearl Harbor, 1-2, 10
Hect, Lieutenant, 154
Heering-Verlag, x
Heifits, Yasha (Jascha Heifitz), 146
Henle, Fritz, x, xvi, xvii, 89
Hina Matsuri (Children's Festival), 106, 110
Hobo, Mr., 141
Honorable Discharge, 162-163
Houston, Rex, 1
Hurricane Hugo, x, xii

— I —

Idaho
  Boise, 25
    Gowen Field, 25
Illinois
  Chicago, 165
  Ft. Sheridan, 162, 165
India, 131
Indiana
  Ft. Wayne, 5
  Technical College, 2, 5
  University Press, 152
Indian Ocean, xv
International Phonetic Alphabet, xi

In the Shadow of Trinity, ix
Irish, 1
Israel, 157
Italian, 99, 101, 133
Italy, 101

— J —

Japan, ix-xi, xv, 1, 32-33, 41, 43-45, 48-49, 52,
    58-61, 71, 76-78, 82, 85, 90, 99, 101-103, 105,
    111, 114, 116, 118, 121, 125, 127, 130-131, 140,
    143-144, 145, 148-149, 151, 155-157, 159, 161,
    166, 168
  Atsugi, 61, 70
    Air Base, 69
  Emporer, xv, 49, 133
  Fussa, 60, 77, 80-82, 143
  Hachioji, 77, 103, 105-111, 157
    Boys Middle School, 104-106
    Gokurakuji Temple, 106
  Hanno, 77, 110-111
    Boys School, 114-115
  Higashifussa, 111
  Hino, 77, 112-114, 157
  Hiroshima, 43-47, 49, 52, 71, 168
  Hokkaido, 67
  Honshu, 61
  Ichigaya, 121, 138-139, 141, 144, 148-149, 151,
    155, 157
  Ie Shima Island, 27, 30, 32-33, 38-39, 41, 43,
    52-55, 57, 59, 61-62, 72, 102, 116, 146
  Iwo Jima, 27, 69-71
  Johnston Island, 27
  Kwajalein Atoll, 27
  Kyoto, 148
  Kyushu, 47
  Meiji
    Imperial Castle, 151-152
    Noh Drama Scenes, 152
  Midway, 27
  Mitaka, 92, 95
  Miyanohira, 120-121, 123, 137-138, 150-151,
    153
  Nagasaki, 43, 47, 49, 52, 168
  Nakano, 99-101
    Society of St. Paul, 99, 101
  Nikko, 110-111
  Okinawa, 26-27, 30, 32-33, 36, 43, 60
    Yontan, 34-35, 53, 62, 69
  Ome, 77-78, 80, 82-85, 118-119, 121-123, 125,
    127-131, 133, 143, 146, 148-149, 154,
    156-158
    Mitake Shinto Shrine, 83-85
  Saipan, 27
  Sakhalin Island, 48
  Sapporo, 67
  Shinjuku, 85, 148
    Station, 86
  Tachikawa, 62, 71-75, 77, 85, 87, 92, 94, 96,
    98, 103, 143, 148, 157

    Air Base, 72
  Tokyo, xv, 47-52, 77, 85-88, 90, 101, 121-123,
    141, 143, 145-146, 148-150, 160
    American Embassy, 88-89
    Bay, 53
    Ginza, 88
    Imperial Hotel, 92
    Imperial Palace, 87, 88
    Machida City, 123-124
    PX (Guinjin Kaikan), 88-89, 91
    Toho Movie Studios, 147-148
    Toho Theatre (The Ernie Pyle Theatre), x,
        89, 90
    Yasukini Shrine, 90-91, 93-94
  Yakota (Fussa City), 77
  Yokasuka, 145
  Yokohama, xv, 47, 73, 75, 145
    Hotel New Grand, 73, 75
  Yokota, 46, 60-65, 67, 69, 70-72, 74, 77-78,
    80-81, 101-102
    Army Air Base, 60, 140
      Reno Tower, 60
  Yotsuya, 101
Japanese (Gook, Jap), xi, xiii, xvii, 27, 29, 30,
    31-33, 38, 43, 45-49, 52-54, 61-62, 67-68, 71,
    75, 77-78, 80-82, 85, 89, 92, 94, 97, 99,
    101-103, 105-106, 108, 110, 114, 116-117, 119,
    121-123, 125, 130-131, 133, 135-137, 139, 140,
    142, 144, 146-148, 150-154, 156-157, 159,
    166-168
  Air Force, 49
  Airplanes
    Betty bombers, 52-55
    Zeroes, 67
  Army, 81, 108
  Artists
    Choshosai, 152
    Kiei, 152
    Ko-Jio, Tsukoka, 152
    Kokuho, Ichiyusai, 152
    Shuntei, 152
    Toyoharu, 152
    Toyokuni, 152
  Diet (Congress), 119
  Government, 52, 114
  House of Peers (Senate), 119, 141, 157
  Music, 140, 143, 146
  Navy, 43, 49
  Railway, 76
    train (densha), 77, 85-86
  Staff, 49, 52
  Surrender team, 52-53, 55-57
Java, 131
Jones, Spike, 26
Joynt, Father, 152, 154

— K —

Kabuki, 152
Kamikaze, 46-47, 52, 60-62, 105

Kansas, 1
Kawabe, General, 52
Keller, Helen, 145
Ketsu-Go, 45
Kikutani
    Namiko, 124
    Taro, xvii, 121-122, 124, 136, 147, 158-159
Korea, 23, 67, 80, 119, 150-151, 156, 165
    Seoul, 66-67
        Kimpo Airdrome, 66-68
Kotatsu, 145
Koto, 140-146
KP (Kitchen Police), 6, 10
Krupp, Corrine, 31
Kutani
    Company, 149
    -ware bowl, 150
    wine cup, 150, 152

— L —
Langford, Frances, 26
Lebanon, 46
Life, x
Lindburg, Ernest W., 16
Lloyd Trestino Line, xv
LORAN, 25
Luzon, 58
    Bataan Peninsula, 32

— M —
MacArthur, General Douglas, 26, 30, 33, 36, 81
MacWilliam, J. H., 20, 23
Manchuria, 131
Marshall Victory, 160-161
Massachusetts, 7
    Boston Museum of Art, 152
    Springfield, 9, 25
        College, 3, 7-8, 10
        Westover Field, 25
Massey, _____, 10
McFarland, Alice, 145
Metrinko, _____, 10
Miami Herald, 47
Michigan
    Detroit, 26
    Sault Ste. Marie, 29
Michio, Miyagi, 143-145
Micronesian Island, 27
    Yap, 27
Midzukami, ix
Miner, _____, 10
Moore, _____, 10
Morse code, 17
Mount
    Fuji, xv-xvi, 78-81
    Mitake, 85
    Suribachi, 27, 71
Mr. (Chef) Jimmy, 73, 75
Murayama dam, 96

Murphy, _____, 10

— N —
Nakajima (Nakashima), 143-145, 157
    Mrs., 139
    Sensai G., 138-141, 145-146
    Yasuko, 138-141, 145-146
Nassau, 25
Nebraska, 1
New Guinea
    Biak, 67, 69-70
New Mexico, ix
    White Sands, 71
    Trinity, ix, 71
New York
    The Bronx, 29
    New York Times, The, x, 90
New Zealand, 38
Noh drama, 146
Norden Bombsight, 25
Nordi (seaweed), 131
Nuclear bomb, 45-46, 168

— O —
Occupation duty, 59, 166-167
Officer's Club (317 Club), 72-75, 80
Ohio, 5
    Carey, xvii, 1-2, 4, 29, 31, 165
        Big Four Train Station, 4
        High School, 2
    Cleveland, 10
    Columbus, 29
    Findlay, 1
    Ft. Hayes, 3-5
    State University, x, 102
Ohn, ix, xiii, 159
Oklahoma, 1
Omezawa, Mr., 103, 114
O'Neill, Jr., Pilot Second Lieutenant Lawrence,
    29, 58
Orient, 131
Oriental
    art, 121, 132, 148-149
    religion, 99, 101
Ozawa, Y., 106

— P —
Pacific, 67, 70
    Theater, 28
Paganini, Father, 99, 102
Paikin, Bombardier Second Lieutenant Jerome,
    29
Palau, 69-70
Paper bomb, 48-49
Pavlovsky, Valentin, 145
Pendleton, Father and Mrs., 9
Pennsylvania
    Philadelphia, 10
Persia, 133

Philippines, 27, 30-32, 34, 57, 70, 99
    Clark Field, 27, 69
    Corregidor Island, 32
    Manila, 11, 30, 31, 56-58
        Bay, 32
    Nichols Field, 30
    St. Anna, 31
Piatigorsky, G., 145
Pilot cadet training
    Advanced Flight, 4, 18, 22
    Basic, 4, 6
    Basic Flight, 4, 16
    Classification, 4, 10-11
    College, 4, 7-9
    Pre-Flight, 4, 11-12
    Primary Flight, 4, 12, 14
    Transition, 4, 25
Pneumonia, 11
P.O.E. (Port of Embarkation), 26
Propaganda, 48, 50-52, 116
Ptomaine poisoning, 9
Pyle, Ernie, 32

— R —

RADAR, 25
Radiation, 43
Red Cross, xv, 10
Rising Sun, The, 48
Rokuby ware, 151
Romberg, Sigmund, 5
Rome, 18
Roosevelt, Eleanor, 67
Rowe, Jeff, x
Russia, xv, 101, 166
Russian, 48, 52, 60, 71, 133, 167
    Navy, 71

— S —

Sakuhachi, 141
Samurai, 152
Sassoon, Sigfried, 1
Schroder, Walter, 145
2nd Combat Cargo Group, 60-61, 71
Semitic, 156-157
Shamisen, 141
Shintoism, 101
Shinto shrine, 90-91
Short snorter, 116
Sino-Japanese War, 152, 156
Smith, Carol, xi
SOS (shit on a shingle), 6
South Carolina
    Charleston Air Base, 25
        Army Air Base, 24-25
Soviets, 166
Spanish, 117
Springfield rifle, 7
Stars and Stripes, 32, 43
Staten Island, 102

Stewart, Basil, 152
St. Lucia Island, 117
Stoney, Lieutenant, 101, 142-144, 152
Suez Canal, xv
Suzaki, Tsuyoshi, 85
Swiss, 1, 112-114

— T —

Tachikawa Stallmen's Association, The New Pro-
    motion of, 94, 97, 106
Taira, Mr., 123
Tait, Lieutenant, 65
Takios, 92
    Mr., 92
    Mrs., 95
Tanner, Audrey, 47
Tarosan, 123, 155
Tea, 78
    ceremony, 78, 150-151
Tench, Colonel Charles T., 60
Tennessee
    Nashville, 3, 10
Texas, 10
Thomas, Jennie M., 145
Thrall, Miss, x
317th Troop Carrier Group, 71
Time, 82
Tirosan, 126, 158
To, 137-138
Tokugawa, 153
Tokugawa, Prince, 134
Tokyo Rose, 32
Toland, John, 48-49, 52
Troop Transport Command, 58
Trumbull, Robert, 90-91
Tsugumo, xvii, 123, 133, 136, 139, 143, 157, 159
    Fujikosan, 122, 142-143
    Mama (Okasan), 78, 121-122, 124, 128, 136,
        152-153, 156, 158-159
    Namikosan, 122-123, 159
        Tairasan, 123
    Papa (Kunetoshi), ix, 49-50, 71, 103, 117-130,
        132, 134-138, 141-144, 146-156, 159
    Totsurosan, 122, 144, 147, 149
Tsu Tsui, Motakazu, 49
Turner, Lieutenant, 92, 95

— U —

United States, 3, 25-26, 29, 43, 47-48, 55, 58,
    70-71, 102, 114, 116, 122, 134
    Government, 52
U.S., 5, 41, 47, 53, 85, 88
    Air Force, xi, 49, 165
    Army, 3, 5, 26, 38, 41, 62, 114, 132, 165
        Enlisted Reserve Corps (ERC), 3
    Army Air Corps, xi, 3, 5-7, 21
        basic training, 3, 6
    Army Air Forces (USAAF), xi, 20-21, 23, 26,
        165

basic training, 7
  Reserve, 165
Coastal Artillery, 5-6, 23
  Anti-Aircraft basic training, 5
  Anti-Aircraft Division, 5
  basic training, 3
Marine, 27, 29, 71
Navy, 10, 26, 39, 41, 49, 62, 64, 70
Utagawa School, 152

— V —

Vaughn, xviii
  Ellen Haffey Piska, xvii
  H. W., T/4, 53
  Jim, xvii, 1, 16
  Joe, xvii, 1
  Margie, *see* Baron
  Mary Lou, xvii
  Paul, xvii, 1
  Robert V., Flight Officer, xiii, xviii, 2, 7, 9-11,
    14-15, 17, 21-22, 24, 29, 35, 37, 42, 44, 50,
    64, 73-75, 83, 87, 91, 95, 100, 122, 125,
    132, 138, 141-142, 156, 159, 161, 163-165,
    168
Vertigo, 19
Veteran's Day (Armistice Day), 133

Vietnam, 23, 165
Virginia
  Ft. Eustis, 3, 5-6
  Lee Hall, 5
Virgin Islands, 49
  St. Croix, x-xi, 10, 49
    Frederiksted, xi
      Estate Carleton, xi
  University of, 85
V-J Day, 53, 55

— W —

Ward, Staff Sergeant, 91
Washington
  Seattle, 160-162
Watanabe, Miss, 141
World War I, 1, 168
World War II, x-xii, 1-2, 8, 23, 30, 47, 90, 157,
  166-168

— Y —

Yamaguchi dam, 96

— Z —

Zeroes, *see* Japanese airplanes